Handbook for Higher Education Faculty

A Framework & Principles for Success in Teaching

By David Garrett Way

NEW FORUMS

NEW FORUMS PRESS INC.

Published in the United States of America
by New Forums Press, Inc.1018 S. Lewis St.
Stillwater, OK 74074
www.newforums.com

Library of Congress Cataloging-in-Publication Data Pending

This book may be ordered in bulk quantities at discount from New Forums Press, Inc., P.O. Box 876, Stillwater, OK 74076 [Federal I.D. No. 73 1123239]. Printed in the United States of America.

ISBN 10: 1-58107-291-0
ISBN 13: 978-1-58107-291-4

Cover art by David Way, "The Veterinary Lecture."

Contents

Introduction

In his very comprehensive piece "Those Who Understand: Knowledge Growth in Teaching" (Shulman, 1986) Lee Shulman lays out his perspective on teacher knowledge—all the various areas of knowledge teachers may draw upon over the course of a teaching career. Besides the obvious area of content knowledge, he adds Pedagogical Content Knowledge: "the most useful forms of representation of those ideas, the most powerful analogies, illustrations, examples, explanations, and demonstrations-in a word, the ways of representing and formulating the subject that make it comprehensible to others"; Curricular Knowledge: "the *materia medica* of pedagogy, the pharmacopeia from which the teacher draws those tools of teaching that present or exemplify particular content and remediate or evaluate the adequacy of student accomplishments" as well as *forms* of knowledge, including propositional knowledge, case knowledge, and strategic knowledge. This is quite an inventory when one steps back to reflect on it all. In the absence of required and formal training and education in pedagogy in higher education, most faculty members may muddle through the practice of teaching touching on these areas of practical knowledge only tacitly. In this book I draw upon Shulman's use of the terms "lore of teaching" and "the wisdom of practice" to represent a continuum of teaching practical knowledge. To me the lore of teaching represents the lower end of the continuum where higher education faculty members are guided by what they observe in their colleagues. With little familiarity in the literature on teaching in higher education a newly appointed faculty member may draw upon this lore out of pure instinct and survival.

On the high end of the continuum is the wisdom accumulated over years of experience. This wisdom may or may not have been informed by a familiarity of the literature in higher education teaching and learning, but it connotes improvement of effectiveness over merely adopting unexamined practices observed in other colleagues. What I have intended in writing this book is to synthesize my own 40 years of teaching experience which includes consulting with hundreds of teachers in higher education on improving their teaching quality and my ever-growing accumulation of knowledge gleaned from reading the research literature in this area. My hope is to help set the beginner on the path to the wisdom of practice as efficiently as possible and to stimulate an interest and curiosity in drawing on and even contributing to the literature base of practical teaching knowledge. The book has been structured to build a framework to guide the practitioner and to encourage their creation of tools that can be effective in guiding practice. Accordingly, I've articulated these tools as principles of teaching at the end of each chapter.

As a reader, I assume you will be teaching something in the near future. You might be a graduate teaching assistant facing your first formal academic instructional task, a post doc who is anticipating moving into a faculty appointment where teaching will be part of your job responsibilities, or a newly hired faculty member with little or no previous teaching experience. On the other hand, you might be a veteran faculty member with years of experience about to design and teach a new course, or seeking effective ways to respond to the patterns found in your students' feedback on their experiences in your courses and with you as an instructor. Whatever your situation, you may have questioned the preparation you have had in learning how to become an effective teacher. Like most academics, your graduate training in whatever discipline you are in would not have required coursework in education or any formal instructional course. What you know may be from workshops you have attended, mentors you may have or simply from observing colleagues. Whatever your background and training in teaching, you wouldn't have picked up this book unless you felt there was something else to learn.

Your situation represents the unique history and culture of higher education. Graduate education has always been about acquiring expertise in a field of knowledge sufficient to empower future faculty members to profess that expertise to others. For generations of faculty members that may have been adequate to get them started. When we compare this approach to elementary and secondary teacher preparation who are required by law to become certified as teachers we may come away feeling satisfied that it does not fully suffice our needs, especially when considering the current criticisms of that system.

But wherever you are in your experience with teaching in the higher education context, the longer you teach, the more it will become apparent that to be truly effective you must continually refine, reflect, adjust and seek input and support. There are many reasons for this professional necessity. The two most obvious have to do with content evolution and societal evolution. Just think how much more we know about biology, physics, genetics, medicine now than even 50 years ago. The social sciences of psychology, sociology, human development, economics and city and regional planning have also been transformed in as many years. In the humanities, consider the changes in literary style, criticism, music, theatre and art over the last century. As long as human society exists, such changes are inevitable and thus we will be constantly creating new courses and updating our curricula in response.

Those of us old enough to recall the world before the internet and handheld technological devices can recognize the changes necessary to accommodate them, let alone the changes in human behavior and interaction they have spurred. But there is even one more major factor in this equation that we must consider in making the argument that professionally, we as teachers must put regular effort into developing our teaching, and that is who we are as individuals. No matter what courses you take, workshops you've attended on teaching, or mentors and exemplars you hope to emulate, in the end you are YOU. Your uniqueness as a human being is the foundation that all your expertise, imagination, risk taking and personal style grow out of.

This notion of identity is worth considering in relation to our professional development and teaching evolution. Questions that may be worth reflecting on are Who are you? What is your core identity that still survives from when you were a young child and that you think helps define you as an individual even now? How are you different now than you were five or ten years ago? If you were to write a vision statement looking into the future 10 or 15 years from now that articulated where you'd like to be in your career, what your life would be like, where you'd like to be working, what your personal life would be like and how it related to your professional life, what would that vision be? To write such a statement would bring you into contact with your personal values. Those values help define who you are—your identity. It is your identity that drives all your decisions: what discipline you have been drawn to, who you associate with, what practical decisions and arguments you make to guide you and justify your path.

Considering who you are and looking at the problems the world is facing currently, how important is teaching and your role as a teacher to you? Do you have some set of over-arching principles that guide you or will guide you as you experiment with new methods, ideas, craft new courses, employ new technologies? If someone was to observe you teach and subsequently ask you why you use PowerPoint, take attendance, give quizzes or use clickers, what compelling arguments can you provide? What are you looking for in your students' performances and development? What guides you in making decisions about how to use class time most effectively? What kind of evidence do you seek to determine to what degree your students are learning what you intend? What is your personal understanding about the relationship between teaching and learning? For that matter, what do you know about learning?

These and other more mundane questions are what may occupy you over a career as a teacher. When we consider what is at stake from our efforts at being and becoming effective teachers it is quite compelling to continually put our best efforts into our practice. What I have come to recognize after 40 years is that generally, it pays to focus first on learning before I consider decisions about teaching approaches. An example will help here: the recent (10-15 years) research in neurobiology in how the brain develops and functions has produced claims that have major implications for educating students. Some of these claims support our own personal experience as learners: that repetition reinforces consolidation of material, that freshmen see the world differently as a group than seniors do. Other research reinforces things we may have believed intuitively: that cognitive learning does not happen in the absence of affect or emotion, supporting our concern and attention to motivation; that our brains retain a plasticity throughout our lives, supporting our emphasis on life-long learning.

When I reflect on what I knew about teaching and learning in 1975 when I had my first teaching position as a graduate TA, I see a person who was focused on teaching more than learning, who was more focused on myself and what I was about than my students and how they might have responded to what I was doing. Teaching to me then was mainly telling. Today, I see my role as a teacher more as an initiator and facilitator of conversations. In my journey between these two perspectives I have experimented and adopted various technologies in my teaching. The most prominent of these has been PowerPoint. Both in my own use of it and having observed hundreds of other examples, I now feel cautious about how and when to use it. I was beginning to feel like it separated me from my students in class like a wall. My current use of it is guided more from what I have learned from experience and research in learning: that whatever new information I have to offer my students, it inevitably will be filtered by what they already know. If I'm trying to teach them the biochemistry of photosynthesis, for example, and some of them believe that photosynthesis shuts down after the sun goes down, that belief may get in the way of their understanding. This understanding about the learning process has dramatically changed how I use PowerPoint. Now, before I even show my first slide, I'll begin with a question like, "When I say 'photosynthesis' to you, what comes to mind?

Beginning a class like this starts a conversation that I can now weave my PowerPoint slides into. It actively engages the students so they are cognitively processing what I have to say and connecting it with their own lives, experiences and prior knowledge. From a neurological perspective, I am helping my students reinforce and build on cognitive frameworks made up of a series of discrete concepts and their interconnecting relationships. Work by educational psychologist David Ausubel and his theory of meaningful learning and educator Joseph Novack and his work with concept mapping have helped me arrive at this principle.

Today, it may not be that surprising that prior knowledge and experience govern the assimilation of new information. But when I observe classrooms throughout the university, I see teaching practices that often ignore this basic principle. In addition, with the advent of the internet and portable computing devices, we are now swimming in a firehose of constantly flowing information that far exceeds our mental capacity to assimilate it all at any one time. Our natural human response to this has been to start filtering that flow. When you sit in the back of classrooms today and observe what students are doing, you might see, besides those shopping on the internet, texting or playing games, students trying to multitask: thinking they can successfully take notes in one computer window while completing an assignment for another course in another.

This is the world we have created for ourselves and what challenges us all as teachers to connect with our students so they can successfully complete our courses by actually retaining and integrating what we teach them, graduate with the knowledge, skills and attitudes to build their lives and careers and to solve the massive and complex world problems they will inherit and have to solve. There is a lot at stake. None of us want to waste our limited and valuable time designing our courses, preparing our classes, assessing our students' learning resulting in an outcome that is superficial and ephemeral.

What will the world be like in another 40 years? That we can't answer, but the question is another major argument for why we can never stop working on developing our teaching and supporting the fundamental role teachers play in society. It is not enough to enter the profession and be guided solely by modeling on what others are doing. Even if what they may be doing appears effective, we can't get away from our identities. What works for one person may just not fit comfortably with who you are. Some new technology may come along, like clickers and you may be tempted as others have, to use them for taking attendance only to find out at the end of the semester that your student evaluations have tanked due to that practice.

This brings us to one last piece of the equation regarding the ever-necessary development of one's teaching practice: reflectivity. Within the stress and competing responsibilities of our roles as teachers it is difficult to have the presence of mind, considering what we know about multi-tasking, to simultaneously monitor and reflect on our actions. A generation ago authors like Donald Schön and Chris Argyris (Schön & Argyris, 1973) were drawing our attention to the importance of being reflective in our professional practices. Now, with the advent of the internet and cell phones, we as a species are plugged in 24/7 to both each other and the growing Googleplex [http://www.rebeccagoldstein.com/publications/plato-googleplex-why-philosophy-won't-go-away]. The idea that to be effective and successful we must wrench our heads out of this firehose of flowing distraction goes against what we have programmed ourselves for. This is a classic learning problem, but on a societal scale. Neuroscience has for decades recognized the limits of our working/short-term memories. There is a cognitive wall we can never get through, but because we have established these behavioral patterns, emotionally, we want to stay with what has become familiar and entrenched. More and more teachers I talk with and more and more literature I read have begun recognizing the fundamental importance of being reflective. Stephen Brookfield's work (Brookfield, 1995) cautions us to be critically reflective by "hunting" our assumptions and using the insights gained thereby to become more aware of ubiquitous power dynamics. Claude Steele's work (Steele, 2010) cautions us to become aware of how stereotype threat can cause not just our minority students, but any of us to be so distracted by characteristics of our identity that it prevents us from performing at our full potential.

But reflectivity necessarily takes time. As teachers we need to educate our students to begin correcting this societal learning problem of continually drinking from the firehose of information. I think of this in terms of a metaphor: the main stream. As humans, we are programmed to want to belong. As growing adolescents, we hunger to belong to the group, to be cool, acknowledged. This is a normal part of growing up at a time when our body's chemistry is demanding it and we are waking to our individuality. At the same time, our brains are forming attitudinal and behavioral patterns before our frontal cortexes are fully developed. Research by William Perry back in the 1970s (Perry, 1970) showed how students' higher order ethical thinking evolves from the age of 18 to 22. Neurobiological research has more recently revealed the frontal cortex doesn't reach completion until around the age of 24 (Brown, Roediger & McDaniel, 2014). By then, in the absence of explicit training and education, individuals have become programmed in ways that makes stepping out of the mainstream of social pressure very difficult.

The problem, as I see it, with being in the main stream of society, whether you are a young, middle-aged or senior adult, is that the massive pressure of the flow carries you along very fast, makes it difficult to pull out due to the insidiousness of peer pressure, difficult to appreciate what landscape is going by so fast and thus difficult to control your destination. But consider and reflect on what happens when you consciously make the effort to move out of the main stream and begin exploring the slower tributaries of life: first you slow down and can better appreciate the local landscape, and second you begin to have a greater sense of control over your destination.

This book has been written and organized to prepare critically reflective teachers to take their place in society and to do that with the knowledge, personal framework and tools to be successful. We'll begin with an exploration of the role of higher education—it's history and development—in influencing society. We'll examine how being critically reflective can serve as a fundamental principle to guide our professional journey. We'll start drawing the underpainting of a self-portrait of our identities to see what anchors us to our unique qualities that set us apart as individuals and will help inform our professional decisions and life-path. Out of our heightened awareness of our identities and experience we'll initiate crafting a framework by which we think and are guided in our teaching practice. We will engage in exercises to flesh out this framework by unpacking our learning experiences and articulating what was previously implicit: our personal theories of teaching and learning.

We'll experiment with ways in which we become more conscious of how our thinking and feelings inform our actions and how this increased consciousness can guide us in creating powerful and compelling learning experiences for our students. We'll look at the changing population of diverse higher education students and how we can build community with them by using our sense of identity as a bridge.

We'll develop artifacts from our academic experiences to serve as benchmarks of our professional development and the major skill areas of teaching: preparing to teach, successfully executing our teaching plans in and out of the classroom to encourage deep and lasting learning in our students, effectively assessing their learning as an authentic process and how to document all these efforts throughout our careers for our own development and in preparation for when we are evaluated by others. I look forward to our collaborative journey together.

References

Argyris, C. & Schon, D. *Theory in practice: Increasing professional effectiveness.* San Francisco: Jossey-Bass, 1974.

Ausubel, D, Novak, J.D, & Hanesian, H. (1978) *Educational psychology – A cognitive view* (2nd ed.). New York: Holt, Rinehart & Winston.

Brookfield, S. (1995). *Becoming a critically reflective teacher.* San Francisco: Jossey-Bass.

Brown, P.C., Roediger III, H.L. & McDaniel, M.A. (2014). *Make it stick – The science of successful learning.* Cambridge, MA: Harvard University Press.

Perry, W (1970). *Forms of intellectual and ethical development in the college years,* San Francisco: Holt Reinhart/Jossey-Bass.

Shulman, L. (1986). Those who understand: Knowledge growth in teaching. *Educational Researcher, 15*(2), 4-14. Washington, DC: The American Educational Research Association.

Steele, C. (2010). *Whistling vivaldi – How stereotypes affect us and what we can do*. New York. Norton.

Chapter 1
Teaching and Identity

Parker Palmer (Palmer, 1998) begins his book, *The Courage to Teach*, with the proposition "We teach who we are." I was struck by the power of this assertion when I first read it. No longer was teaching just an act about some subject, but it had become an expression of self. I reflected on my own experience with some of the teachers in my life: Mr. Romans, my very tall and imposing 6th grade teacher who disciplined students in his class by putting them over his knee and spanking them in front of their classmates; Mr. Rosato, my senior high school history teacher who worked as a bricklayer in the summers and was a Teddy Roosevelt enthusiast, and, of course my parents: my father who was a first generation college student from a poor upstate New York family and my mother, the daughter of a dentist who put himself through dental school by playing the violin. Each of these teachers practiced instructing out of their unique identities. After many years of teaching myself, I recognize that it is impossible for anyone to teach without the influence of their identity. This may seem self evident, but in my experience working with teachers over the years, rarely do they go about beginning to do it by recognizing explicitly how their identity will influence that process.

Instead, their focus is on what they will teach and the techniques available to convey that content. As time goes by, they will recognize certain behavioral tendencies that are driven by their personal tolerance for risk-taking, comfort with certain technologies, or socialized attitudes and approaches modeled by others but that fit comfortably within their behavioral repertoire. To me, what distinguishes the average teacher from those I consider masters includes personal characteristics like perseverance, courage, a strong commitment to consciously-held core values, and above all, a conscious set of principles learned from experience that drive their decisions that they can articulate—they know and can explain the reasons why they do what they do. These reasons, that they might explain to someone else who might observe their teaching, have grown out of who they are.

So, this brings us to the question of the nature of identity. Upon reflection, we might think identity is static: we will always be ourselves. Imprisoned in our uniqueness, we may lament our shortcomings and experience frustration that we can't emulate our pedagogical heroes. I remember vividly working with a young graduate teaching assistant in biology many years ago during my own graduate work. I had made a video recording of him teaching a laboratory session and his reaction when we reviewed the video together was, "I'm not flamboyant enough." I asked him to explain what he meant and he said "I'd like to be like Johnny Carson." Not withstanding the antiquity of his request back in the late '70s, if you knew Steve, you'd know there was no Johnny Carson in him. So, in one respect, our identity is "locked": we remain who we are. However, on the other hand, if you reflect back on your identity at the age of five years compared to your present age, you'll realize you have changed. The five-year-old is still there, but you've added much experience and many bodily cells since then.

Why is identity important at this point in time? I see two compelling reasons for anyone's success in life. First, to be successful at whatever you aspire to do—like teach others—knowing who you are and how your unique identity is expressed in your work can help provide an enhanced sense of control and efficiency. Once Steve realized he was never going to be "like Johnny Carson" he could more productively take inventory and ownership of his existing qualities and skills to gain more confidence in his teaching efforts. A more contemporary reason to focus on identity has to do with current societal norms that newer technology has inspired. Someone once referred to this phenomenon as "praying mantis people"—the hunched over, close-to-the-shoulder-hands of us as we walk along with our texting devices—constantly plugged in to the social network. To someone like myself who came to cell phones late in life and who has set boundaries for myself and my digital devices, this need to be constantly plugged in to others remains optional at best and detrimental more than likely. What happens to one's sense of individuality under these circumstances? Who is likely to take the time to step back, reflect on whatever is transpiring and its consequences, under these conditions? For those who have grown up with it, it is the norm. But what price is being paid for all those other things that may more profitably occupy our consciousness? What patterns of thought and behavior are becoming dominant in the lives of young people who will need to be able to recognize themselves as separate from this social consciousness enough to compete in the search for a job and career path that fits who they are?

The title of Palmer's book, *The Courage to Teach*, should give a novice pause to consider there may be sources of fear in undertaking such a career path. I can't put a number to the times in my own teaching experience and from those teachers I've worked with where fear was a dominant part of the experience. In fact, there is a professor I know who has had over 30 years of experience who confided to me that when he began, he was "terrified" of teaching. He went on to say that now after so many years, he's still terrified! Now it seems to me that all new teachers can be expected to begin with a sense of trepidation and anxiety. The impostor syndrome is a common experience. If, however, one aspires to reach a point in practice where one's anxiety is to become manageable, to reach a point even where teaching be-comes a source of energy rather than a drain of energy, it seems a necessary ingredient that one believes enough about oneself to have the courage to push on through the fear.

Think about this just from a very practical point of view: you have spent years accumulating a body of knowledge you wish to profess. The first time you go to express this to others the words coming out of your mouth may not flow just right (think of a graduate A exam). You may stumble and pause as you search for just the right words. This makes you self conscious, which in turn may make you more flustered. Your voice drops and you sound hesitant even about this topic you felt so much an authority on. If this sounds familiar—join the club! It happens to all of us. A close faculty friend of mine, someone I've followed throughout his teaching career over 25 years, from a young assistant professor to his current status as a full professor has won numerous teaching awards. When he comes to share his teaching journey with my students, he begins by sharing a scene from the Peter Sellers film, "Being There" where the character of Chauncey Gardner sits with the President of the United States and his senior advisor guilelessly leaving the impression he's an economic savant, when in fact, he's simply a gardener. My professor friend tells my students that he still feels like a similar impostor whenever he talks to anyone about teaching.

Fortunately for most of us, and even my friend and others who frequently feel anxious at the prospect of teaching, we get over our initial fears and over time and experience the words coming out of our mouths more closely link with the thoughts in our heads we are trying to convey to others. Our voice becomes more confident and loud and our attention shifts away from ourselves to our audience. I call this "finding your voice" and it is a predictable phenomenon in all teachers' developmental journeys.

There is another critical aspect of the juncture of one's identity and the experience of fear that all teachers must be alert to and that grows out of the work by Claude Steele on identity threat. The situation I was just describing of teachers' fears preventing their effective functioning can happen in many other contexts. The most relevant for teachers is where our students experience a threat during an academic task of high consequence, like a test, and that threat is directly related to their identity. The examples he gives are women who go in to a math test with the awareness of the stereotype that women are not as good at math as men, or it could be an African-American student facing a similar task with the heightened sensitivity of the stereotype of their racial identity at not having the potential to perform well at such a task. As Steele explains, it is the threat that any of us might experience due to certain characteristics of our identity that serves as a sufficient distraction from performing the task, resulting in our underperformance of our true potential.

So, these ubiquitous factors like our identity and human capacity for experiencing fear are very relevant to effective teaching. It is therefore necessary to begin considering some other fundamental aspects of life that come into play if one aspires to be an effective teacher. What comes to mind is the very natural way we learn through modeling. In the absence of any kind of formal training in pedagogy, like a certification program, course work or workshops, most higher education teachers have tended to model their practice on others' examples. Even in a more formal mentoring relationship, a novice teacher may be learning from an experienced veteran who himself learned his practice through trial and error and who's knowledge base is limited to what Lee Shulman (Shulman, 1986) has called the "lore of teaching." If I was to summarize the trajectory of higher education teaching over the past 30-40 years, I'd say we have been slowly moving away from a dominance of lecturing to what some have referred to as "active learning" (Bonwell & Eisen, 1991) teaching methods. With the advent of the internet, academics have become aware that spending time in class presenting information that is constantly available on-line is no longer necessary. Knowing as we all do from experience the power of active cognitive and emotional engagement with what we intend to learn, higher education teachers are spending more class time crafting and facilitating learning activities. This is very promising and rewarding—when it is done effectively.

Whether you approach teaching by trying to emulate certain models, have worked with a mentor, or simply go about it by trial and error, your approach is a reflection of your identity. What does your existing repertoire of choices consist of? Is it limited to lecturing versus discussing? Lecturing is still such a prevalent teaching method that some of both my students and faculty colleagues use the terms lecturing and teaching synonymously. To me, to do so is a reflection of how they think about teaching—part of what some might call their "teaching philosophy." Will confounding teaching and lecturing be a problem? To find out, let's step back and consider an analogy.

The analogy I'd like to propose that grows out of our earlier consideration of the importance of identity in teaching is this: *teaching is to lecturing as being is to doing.* Think about that for a moment. What, in your mind, is the relationship between teaching and lecturing? What is the difference between being and doing? Some may consider these differences/distinctions negligible, others may see them as considerably distinct. However you may personally see these relationships, lets examine this analogy more closely.

If teaching is a larger concept that encompasses much more than lecturing, following from the analogy, being is a much larger concept than doing. When I've raised this distinction with my students, their initial reaction is confusion: how can I do something without being? Isn't doing things what occupies most of our time as human beings? Why is such a distinction important? I was first alerted to the significance of this distinction when I was reading some counseling literature that raised the question, "Are we human beings or are we becoming human doings?" When I thought about that, it seemed that a human doing had a negative ring to it, that if all I was spending my time was in the doing of things, my sense of being might be diminished. Similarly, if all I did as a teacher was to lecture, I would be living in a very limited world and my potential for connecting with my students would be equally restricted. Making choices where we go beyond what is familiar, like lecturing, to extend our learning as human beings is a reflection of our identity. When we're new to something we tend to gravitate to choices where we feel more in control. Lecturing, compared to engaging with a group of students interactively, puts us more in control. However, we are all familiar with having conversations with people. The movement in higher education teaching away from lecturing as the dominant form to more actively engaging with students in class means we must be willing to give up some of the control and the relative security associated with that. When one recognizes the familiarity and comfort associated with a stimulating conversation, we may be more willing to move in that direction.

This path towards more engagement with students in teaching is supported by much work in learning theory and neurobiology (Brown, et al., 2014; Dweck, 2008; Zull, 2002)). Looking at the physiology of the brain, we have come to understand that learning is a process of repeated firings between brain cells. When certain neuronal networks are triggered repeatedly over time, they physically enlarge, becoming stronger and more dominant. In addition, when we begin to make new connections between brain cells and repeatedly recall those connections, they grow stronger and therefore more easily accessed. This is something we all can recognize from experience. Think of something you do regularly and often, like go from your home to your place of work. When this path was first established, you might have had to take time to look for and remember landmarks to guide you successfully to your destination. But after even a short period of time, this path became so routinized that you no longer had to consciously think about it. Now think of a time when you might have had to stop off somewhere on your way to work, breaking your learned, routinized regimen. You may very well have passed your goal before remembering you had to make this detour.

So, as we all know from experience, learning takes place over time. This is why simply telling something to someone doesn't mean they've actually learned it. So why is it we still spend so much of our time doing that in our teaching? To answer that question, we must move from the perspective of an individual learning something, to the perspective of our species' learning something. To explain what I mean, consider the photograph below of an archeological dig in Alexandria Egypt (http://www.crystalinks.com/cd.html). It shows a classroom dating back to over 300 BC. One could imagine Euclid or Ptolemy teaching here. This structure put the teacher at the center of everything in a time before printed and widely available books, when the transfer of information required note taking. Lecturing has become embedded in our human consciousness so long that, throughout the world, millions of human beings attend them every day.

Which brings us back to being: as pointed out earlier, once we repeatedly do something enough times, doing it becomes so familiar, we don't think about it as consciously as we once had to when it was new. If you've attended as many lectures as even a freshman will have by the end of their first year in college, the thrill may have evaporated and the focus necessary to retain what was conveyed may no longer exist. Now, add to that another aspect of our contemporary human society that is making lecturing an even stronger relic of our human past: the internet and our portable devices that allow us to plug into it whenever we have a mind to. In my work, I have spent a lot of time sitting in the back of other people's classes as an observer at the request of the instructor with the purpose of helping them improve their teaching. What I invariably see, not only in large lecture halls but even in small interactive language classes of no more that eight students is students texting each other under the table, or watching football games, playing computer games, shopping, etc.

Young people today who have been born into this river of flowing exchange, as even we older folks who have grown to become part of it ourselves, are learning to filter out those parts of the flow that either don't immediately seduce our attention, or seem irrelevant to our current purposes. Knowing what we now know about the learning process, this scenario seems a very costly waste of many people's time. Academics like Eric Mazur (Mazur, 1997) at Harvard, Carl Wieman at Stanford, and other liberated faculty members here at Cornell are choosing to use their very limited and precious class time more productively. Recognizing these current distractions to our students' attention it is instructive to contrast the practice of lecturing to an ancient teaching method that is still used with some regularity today, although not always effectively: the Socratic method. What is compelling about this approach is its use and engagement with the student's prior knowledge and the seemingly equivalency of roles between teacher and student: the teacher (Socrates) asks the student (Meno) to tell him what he thinks virtue is (http://classics.mit.edu/Plato/meno.html). This begins a conversation that forces Meno to explore what he thinks he knows and to justify his understanding of it.

So now we have two teaching strategies on the table: lecturing and the Socratic dialogue. Going back to Palmer's assertion that we teach who we are, it seems useful for each one of us to reflect on who we are and the experiences we've had that may establish the beginnings of our unique teaching philosophy, whatever strategies they may include. If someone were to throw you—sink or swim—into a classroom of students with the responsibility to teach them, what would you do? How would you prepare? How would you use the limited time available to you? Would you use any form of technology, like PowerPoint? And if so, how would you use it? What principles might guide you in developing your slides? The content itself? Other examples of PowerPoint presentations? If someone were to make a video recording of your class and you watched it back, what would you see? Vestiges of other teachers in your life: your high school science teacher? Your mother? With no prior experience, in this scenario you would be drawing on experiences that define who you are. So, I suggest that the prior knowledge and experience you were drawing on constitute an unarticulated, unstructured, tacit personal theory of teaching and learning. Something was there before you were put into that situation. What was it? Could you explain it to one of your students who might ask?

You may not think you have a "personal theory of teaching and learning" but I suggest that as a human being, you do. It has been developing on a subconscious level all your life. I will always remember an experience I had as a five-year old with my dad. We were in the kitchen and he had just made himself a cup of tea. We were standing by the still red hot electric stove burner and I looked at it and asked him, "Is that hot?" He said, without much forethought, "Touch it and find out." Now my dad was a world war II veteran who saw duty on Guam not too many years before this exchange between us. His own father had been a school teacher in up-state New York, teaching in a one-room school house. My dad's approach to teaching me came out of his identity as well as his previous experiences. I can't help but think he must have thought many times after I burned myself that morning of more effective ways of teaching me what I needed to learn.

Of course as we both grew older after that experience, we both continued to learn and experiment with more refined ways to teach and learn from each other. Our personal theories continued to develop as our identities evolved with our accumulating experience. For anyone beginning teaching, you may be wondering what do I mean by a "personal theory of teaching and learning?" Let's start with theory: a theory has been described as growing out of empirical observations of phenomena. Theories are a means of organizing ideas and making sense of our observations. Stephen Brookfield has said "Theory is the productive enemy of premature certainty." So, as we continually gain more teaching experience, we are learning how certain things relate to each other: "getting burned is something you will not forget." My father made a decision (maybe not too carefully) that by suggesting I do something, I might learn what I wanted to know. This connects the act of teaching with the experience of learning. Teachers teach so their students can learn—otherwise why are they necessary? I could have learned the same thing without my father's prodding. The "personal" aspect of such theories implies that we each have one and that it is unique to us as an individual—that it is tied to our identity.

My work with teachers over the years as well as my own teaching experience has helped me understand the components of an individual's personal theory of teaching and learning. They consist of two parts: concepts of teaching, and principles of teaching. My mentor, D. B. Gowin, (Gowin, 1981) used to say, "A concept is a sign or symbol pointing to a regularity in events." The act of teaching is a series of events starting with our preparation to teach and extending through our performances in the classroom and the experiences we create and share with our students that extend even after the class is over. It has been said that all teaching is a series of empirical, on-the-spot experiments. There is much truth in that statement. For the novice, with little previous experience, operating from exemplary models from other effective teachers may be the first step. Over time, as strategies are employed and refined, we gradually build a repertoire of approaches. Very often we end up having to make the same mistakes over again many times before we recognize the limits of certain approaches within various contexts and with a diversity of individuals. What makes effective teaching complicated are the vast number of variables involved. Even something that has been proven to be effective repeatedly is not guaranteed to work every time. How can we make sense of this complexity?

The work of my two mentors, D. B. Gowin and Joseph Novak has helped me answer that question. Using Gowin's definition of what a concept is and recognizing what Novak means when he says, "We think with concepts" we can begin to sort out all the vast complexity of teaching and its relationship with learning. To conceptualize something—a recognized regularity in events—is to give a name to it. One example is "warming up." I use this term to refer to what happens in any class within the first 5 to 10 minutes. What regularity am I referring to? Anyone who teaches knows that it takes time to get everyone's attention, to get the class focused on the subject at hand and to build a sense of connection between the instructor, students and topic of the day. This does not happen right away, it takes some time. Effective teachers recognize this and have what I call principles of teaching to address this regularity. An example from language instruction can help: language instructors know that their students must learn to think in the target language—they can't get by continually translating everything and function well. So they engage their students individually as they enter the classroom, even before formal instruction begins, in the target language, but in a limited but familiar vocabulary: "Bonjour! Comment allez vous?" A principle, in Gowin's terms "is a guide to action." As teachers engage with their students and course material, they must continually make decisions. Conscious principles are useful in effectively dealing with the myriad events that transpire in the act of teaching. In the absence of such consciousness, we are just experimenting and hoping things work out. This is not to conflict with the assertion that all teaching is a series of on-the-spot empirical experiments, just to say that to gain more of a sense of control, and thus confidence in one's actions and efficacy, building a toolbox of principles of teaching can be very empowering.

Let's take another example: "checking for understanding." That's another concept of teaching teachers regularly engage in. The most familiar form it takes as an action is to stop one's delivery of content and ask the question, "Are there any questions?" Usually this comes at the last minute in the class. How many times have you seen a teacher end a class with the question, "Are there any questions?" What usually happens? In my experience, usually the students begin packing up to leave. What if we were to move that same prompt to an earlier time in the class, say after the first 20 minutes or half an hour? What has your experience been with that scenario? The many classes I've observed over the years in many disciplines has revealed that students most often sit there with blank stares at the instructor. What is happening here?

First, from a conceptual point of view, it makes every bit of sense that a teacher frequently check for understanding of the material covered by their students. We know that the human short-term memory can only hold so many ideas at the same time (Miller, 1967). Making sure what we have covered has been understood before adding more content to that memory makes a lot of sense. However, from a principle of teaching point of view, simply stopping suddenly and asking, "Are there any questions?" has regularly proven not to work very well. In my experience observing teachers, this question is frequently asked accompanied by certain conflicting behaviors: the instructor looking at their watch, or turning around and erasing the board, breaking eye contact—and most frequently—waiting only a second, or even less before beginning to speak again. So, we have a concept of teaching—checking for understanding—and a corresponding principle of teaching: stop periodically and ask, "Are there any questions?" However, our experience has shown us that employing that principle is likely to be ineffective. To extend and further refine one's personal theory of teaching and learning, given this insight, we must create an alternative or additional principle of teaching for the concept of checking for understanding. My experience has shown me there are three components to creating an effective checking for understanding principle: making eye contact, leaving sufficient wait time, and the verbal prompt used. So, a more effective principle that teachers are currently using with more frequency to deal with the concept of checking for understanding is the "Think-Pair-Share." Conceptually, this principle—or strategy if you will—is listed in a book of "Classroom Assessment Techniques" co-written by Pat Cross and Tom Angelo (Cross & Angelo, 1993). What distinguishes it from the bankrupt "Are there any questions?" approach is the necessity by the instructor to craft a specific content-based question as part of their preparation for the class, at a time when they can make sure the question prompt is clear and focussed enough to provide sufficient validation by students' responses that in fact, they do understand what has been covered. So, that addresses the verbal prompt criterion. The wait-time criterion is addressed effectively by the fact that the instructor tells the students they have a time limit (1-3 minutes, depending on the difficulty of the prompt and the amount of time they have for the activity.) What makes this principle/strategy even more powerful is that it engages the students in another concept: cooperative learning. By instructing the students to first think of a response to the prompt, and then share their response with a partner, the students have the opportunity to learn from each other—either be validated by knowing someone else has the same or similar response, or be alerted to the fact that either there is more than one response, or maybe their response is incorrect.

So, we can see how there are concepts of teaching we can build by putting names to the regularities in teaching and learning events we experience as teachers, and how, to be useful, we need to craft principles of teaching based on them in order to gain more control over the complex variables in teaching and to become more effective in our intentions. Other prominent and ubiquitous concepts of teaching include motivation, feedback, assessment, preparation, being accessible and present, and empathy. How an individual addresses each of those concepts through principled actions inevitably grows out of their unique identity. That is a most liberating thought since it is a recognition that there is no one way to teach and that each of us will naturally develop what may be considered our own personal *style* of teaching growing out of who we are as unique human beings.

Principles from Chapter 1:

1. Articulate your reasons for why you do what you do, both for yourself and for your students.
2. Begin by taking inventory of who you are: your values, fears, and tolerance for change.
3. Teaching goes beyond telling to generating conversations.
4. Generate concepts of teaching by giving names to the regularities or patterns in teaching events to help you think more explicitly about teaching and your individual style.
5. Generate principles of teaching that serve to guide actions that apply to identified teaching concepts, which together are your evolving personal theory of teaching and learning.

References

Angelo, T. A., & Cross, K. P. (1993). *Classroom assessment techniques* (2nd ed.). San Francisco: Jossey-Bass

Brown, P.C., Roediger III, H.L. & McDaniel, M.A. (2014). *Make it stick – The science of successful learning.* Cambridge, MA: Harvard University Press.

Brookfield, S. (1995). *Becoming a critically reflective teacher.* San Francisco: Jossey-Bass.

Dweck, C. (2006). *Mindset – The new psychology of success.* New York: Ballantine.

Gowin. D.B. (1981). *Educating.* Ithaca, NY: Cornell University Press.

Palmer, P. (1998). *The courage to teach: Exploring the inner landscape of a teacher's life.* San Francisco: Jossey-Bass.

Miller, G.A. (1967). The magical number seven, plus or minus two: Some limits on our capacity for processing information. In *The Psychology of Communication.* New York: Penguin.

Zull, J. E. (2002). *The art of changing the brain.* Sterling, VA: Stylus.

Chapter 2

Reflection and Teaching

All teachers reflect—we can't help it. You spend time working out a plan you think will be effective, then carry it out with your students and even as you're walking out the door of the classroom, what are you doing: thinking to yourself how well did it go? Did they get it? Did you hold their attention? Were your examples effective? How about your slides? How were you feeling—connected with the class, or too wrapped up in your own head and agenda? What will you do different next time? This chapter is about what reflective teaching is, how to productively go about it and how to build it into your teaching routine throughout your career.

Even though teaching may compel us to dwell on how well we're doing, productive reflection is more complex than that. Let's go back to the idea that we all have a personal theory of teaching and learning. Work done at Harvard in the 1970s by Chris Argyris and Donald Schön (Argyris & Schon, 1974) can be helpful and instructive here. They suggested we each have two working theories operating simultaneously: *our espoused* theory and our *theory in use*. Our espoused theory operates hypothetically when we consider something *a priori*. How would I respond if one of my students came to see me in office hours and tried to manipulate me into raising his grade on an exam? In contrast to this is our theory in use: if we were to make a video recording of my actual exchange with that student in a way that wouldn't influence it, we would be witnessing my theory in use. So, in effect, Argyris and Schön are distinguishing between what we say we do, on the one hand, and what, in fact, we do on the other.

This distinction is both very important and useful. If, over time, I am recognizing that fewer and fewer of my students are coming to me in office hours and I am concerned about that and want to try and reverse the trend, exploring both how my intentions (espoused theory) are influencing my actions (in-use theory) and how an analysis of my actions over time might inform how I think about that aspect of teaching could prove helpful in accomplishing my goal. The important thing here is the realization that, by and of themselves, neither our espoused theories nor theories-in-use should always take precedence. As Donald Schön has said in his seminal book *The Reflective Practitioner* (Schön, 1983), there is knowledge in our actions. As we explored in the previous chapter, if I have an implicit, unarticulated and unexamined personal theory of teaching and learning, so long as I never examine it, make it explicit and put it into words, professionally I am left in the world of trial and error. My learning curve about teaching will be shallower and longer, characterized by making the same mistakes repeatedly until I become conscious enough of them to recognize the need to change. Equally however, there may be wisdom in my actions that upon examination, can productively inform my espoused theory. Even further, we all have had the experience of having a strong conviction about something (espoused) , but over time are continually disappointed that we have yet to successfully put into action that espoused conviction (in use).

Imagine periodically having a dialogue between your espoused theory and theory in use. It might go something like this:

Espoused Theory (ET)—I believe strongly in giving my students room to articulate their thinking about the subject matter in class so I can effectively monitor if they are learning what I intend.

Theory-in-Use (TIU)—But what happened in class today was you started talking, got excited and energized and totally dominated class time, resulting in little input from the class. Do you remember that time when you had your students give group presentations on the week's readings? They did most of the talking and you were still able to come in with helpful reinforcing and focusing comments.

ET—That's right but that meant there were a number of ideas I thought were critical that we never ended up exploring. I think next week I'll follow up the in-class group presentation with an on-line discussion board exchange of the points I think were glossed over.

TIU—Sounds like a plan. Let's do it!

This kind of reflective thinking about events that have already transpired is what Schön referred to as "reflecting-on-action." I have spent many hours over the years reviewing video recordings I made of both my students and faculty members teaching their classes. We then sit down—hopefully within 24 hours—and review the recording together. My role in this process is to facilitate the teacher to reflect on their teaching actions. We can both recognize what went successfully—where skill was exercised by the teacher—and when things went less well and there was room for revisions in both thought and actions for the future.

Obviously, my goal is not to follow everyone around with a video camera, but through a few powerful moments of behavioral analysis and reflection, to stimulate the teacher to begin doing what Schön referred to as "reflection-in-action." The assumption and hope is that if someone spends enough time becoming familiar with reflecting *on* action, they can more readily begin reflecting *in* action. This brings us back to the notion of teaching as a continual series of on-the-spot empirical experiments. If, through my efforts at reflecting on my teaching through work with a mentor or teaching consultant, or by analyzing records I make of my teaching actions and thinking through a journal I have kept over time, I can learn to recognize patterns that require modification, or can create new scripts to more successfully carry out my espoused intentions. I now have a means to consciously and continually develop and refine my teaching practice throughout my career.

Some may question whether there is a point of no return in this process: that after so many years teaching the same thing, or simply after a certain period of time I may reach a point where no further modification is necessary and thus no need for further reflection. But consider this: how has the advent of the internet, laptop computers and software like PowerPoint changed how we teach? Imagine 20 years from now: I doubt we can even imagine all the new innovations that may come along by then that will make both our current thinking and teaching practice obsolete! Consider as well how society changes in general. Issues and norms evolve. Economic forces influence our values and focal points. I would therefore suggest it is necessary for every teacher to continually work on developing their teaching throughout their career.

If that is a professional imperative, how can a very busy academic use their time most wisely in continually updating and modifying their teaching reflectively? One very seductive approach is to rely mainly on technology and newer technologies as they come along to serve the purpose of instructional development. Let's take the example of PowerPoint to see why too much of a reliance on technology might not entirely serve our reflective purposes. From the point of reflectivity, the use of technology in teaching is a means—ends issue. My experience and recommendation for anyone considering adopting any kind of technology use for teaching is to start with your instructional goals: what are you wanting to achieve? When PowerPoint came along a number of years ago, instructors had been using overhead projectors and transparent slides to present course material. Of course, this approach still reflected the dominance of lecturing as a preferred teaching method. Just from a technology point of view, moving away from transparencies, which were costly and not environmentally friendly, to using PowerPoint on a laptop made a lot of sense. But look where this transition has lead us: student attendance has dropped in classes where the instructor has relied too heavily on PowerPoint and providing copies of slides on-line so students can download them without the need to attend class. Instructors are still creating passive classroom learning experiences for their students because they're using that time to cover course content exclusively through PowerPoint. Now students are tuning out with their own laptops and being distracted by other things they can be doing with their devices. So, to back up and reflectively process this situation more effectively, the first question might be, "What is the instructor trying to achieve?" If they are focusing more on stimulating the students' learning rather than limiting themselves to just thinking about teaching as content delivery, they might come up with the idea to post their content notes using PowerPoint on the web, require students to post their own responses/questions about that content before they come to class, and then use class time more productively by engaging with students in a series of learning activities. This is what has been referred to as "flipping the class" (Bretzmann, 2014).

My experience has been that higher education faculty members rely too heavily on the promise of technology to develop their teaching. This may seem like an easy fix. However, one faculty member I've known for years and followed his teaching development over a 25 year period bought into using PowerPoint to teach his classes and after investing a huge amount of time developing his course slides, has come to realize it was not the best use of his time. My own use of PowerPoint as a teaching tool has diminished considerably over the years. I find it separates me too much from my students and limits my need to periodically interact spontaneously with them when either I or they need to interact. Once you've put together a PowerPoint presentation, it becomes a script for your class. I've come to integrate interactive exercises within my PowerPoint slides as a means of helping my students integrate the material I've covered during the presentation. In other words, PowerPoint is a means to an end (my students learning) rather than an end in itself (cover a certain amount of material.)

Stephen Brookfield's work on critical reflection (Brookfield, 1995) is a rich source on both the importance and nature of reflection in teaching. One of the focal points he suggests is "hunting assumptions." We all make assumptions continually. The problem is, in the absence of consciously reflecting on them, they recede into the background of our awareness. I may look out at my students in class, see one with what appears to be a disgruntled or even angry look on her face and assume I or my teaching are the cause. Parker Palmer describes a similar experience with a student he had he refers to as "the student from hell." It turned out that what Palmer assumed was a look directed at him and stimulated by his behavior was in fact due to something entirely different (Palmer, 1998).

Probably the biggest mistake most faculty members make in their teaching grows out of their assumptions about what students can reasonably assimilate either in a single class or even a semester-long course. We tend to cram too much material into the limited time we have with our students. As I have taught the same courses and material over the years, the most consistent effort I make in revising them is to cut out unnecessary readings and topics. This effort has paid off greatly in reduced complaints by students about workload and perceived irrelevancy and freed us all up to engage with the remaining material on a deeper level.

Probably the biggest source of student anxiety in any course is how they will be evaluated and graded. This can create all kinds of dysfunctional interactions between individual students and their teachers. I've seen many courses that are designed around the practice of scheduling two prelim exams and a final. The instructor may have modeled this practice on courses they had taken as a student or on colleagues' suggestions or policies. The assumption here may be that this way of assessing student learning will be sufficient to measure students' learning and be acceptable since they may be familiar with it. But stepping back reflectively, looking at this scenario from the students' point of view gives the teacher room for insight into possible problems and solutions to those problems. I think of assessment as data points. How many data points do I need to measure the students' evolving learning? How many data points will they need to feel comfortable and confident they know how well they're doing without weighting any one assessment too highly to create undue stress? How about other means of assessment besides exams? Within the context of the subject matter, how will the students be assessed on this knowledge once they get out of school? And who will be doing the assessing?

Another area where teachers' assumptions frequently lead them astray has to do with their relative cognitive, critical thinking and intellectual abilities. Work done back in the 1970s by

William Perry (Perry, 1970) showed differences in how incoming freshmen view the world and process information compared to when they become seniors four years later. Anyone raising children has seen these differences: freshmen are more likely so see the world in a dualistic, right/wrong, black/white point of view. They are more willing to accept things at face value—less likely to question sources of information. After four years of college, they begin to appreciate the world is much more complicated: some problems have no one correct solution; over their college years our students begin to recognize the necessity for responsibly making commitments to various problem solutions and issues.

More recent research in neurobiology (Asato, Terwilliger, Woo & Luna, 2010) has shown that the frontal cortex of our brains take longer to fully develop than what was previously thought—that they may not be fully developed until after the average student has graduated from college. This research has revealed that the frontal cortex is responsible for impulse control, consideration of behavioral consequences, ethical decision making and goal setting. As more mature adults, higher education faculty members making decisions based on assumptions of students' capabilities in these areas may be discouraged by students' relative performance.

This leads us to the second most critical aspect of Brookfield's work in critical reflection: the influence of power in distorting our intentions and impacts on students. There is no question that in the relationship between the role of teacher and that of student, there is a power differential. There is no escape from this fact. As teachers, we know things our students don't but want them to learn. We have the responsibility to make sure that they exit our courses educated about what the course was about and that the process of educating them is benign in nature. At the same time, we all are human beings and thus have human imperfections. Power dynamics between teachers and students go both ways. I have found the reflections of Parker Palmer very helpful when considering the role and nature of power in teaching. Palmer asks, "What is the source of my power as a teacher? Does it emanate from within me or is its source outside of me?" (Palmer, 1998, pp.

32-33) When I reflect on that question from my own experience, I realize my source of power emanates out of the quality of the relationship I have established with my students, both collectively and individually—that it comes from outside. Anyone who has taught recognizes the differences in connections with individual students. If, in the act of teaching a class I look out and see a certain percentage of them dozing off or not paying attention, my sense of power dissipates. If I have students who don't attend class regularly or don't invest sufficiently in my course, I feel a loss of power to influence their learning. So, to disregard power in teaching is to abdicate a certain part of our responsibility as teachers.

Palmer's exploration of power in teaching is constructively contrasted with his reflections on authority. Again, he asks, "What is the source of my authority as a teacher, does it reside inside of me or emanate from somewhere outside of myself?" For me, this question helped me to the realization that my sense of authority comes from within—it is generated by the quality and depth of my knowledge of the subject matter I teach. In the last chapter we explored the impostor syndrome and how, with experience, we find our voices as teachers. If I am put in the position, as some higher education faculty are sometimes, of having to teach something relatively new to me (Huston, 2009), my sense of authority is eroded.

As exemplary learners for our students, we have a responsibility to model effective and efficient reflectivity and learning. I believe this means we must be concerned beyond simply sharing our expertise in terms of knowledge, but spend time sharing the way we think and process the knowledge we have and are building as scholars in our fields. An example here will help. Traditionally, high computational subjects like mathematics, physics and engineering have focused on solving quantitative problems in course assessments. That makes sense since that is what people in those disciplines spend a lot of time doing. Work comparing novice problem solvers with experts (Larkin, McDermott, Simon and Simon, 1980) has shown the differences between their respective levels of skill. Anyone who has taught in these areas has seen the tendency of students to want to "get the correct answer" (often as fast as possible—especially on a long exam.) An engineering professor I know has started teaching his classes in a different way to allow exchanges between him and his students about the ways they are thinking about problem solving while they are in the act. He has them pair up and solve problems collaboratively on the blackboard. This frees him up to go around the class, listen in and observe what they are writing on the board, ask them questions about their reasoning and solution strategies. In these exchanges he can raise questions, offer prompts, ask for clarifications and provide insights—all of which expose their relative thinking to open examination and reflection. This example shows how simply getting the correct answer is not sufficient to become an expert problem solver. Experts think differently in the process of solving problems. For them, it is not so much about the answer that occupies them, but the process of arriving at answers that is important. If they intend to impart that expertise to their students, they have to 1) be aware of that expertise, 2) be able to articulate it and impart it effectively and then 3) be able to effectively assess their students' developing skills by eliciting the necessary evidence of it. This will require going beyond just looking at the final answer, but taking the time to review and comment on the thinking employed in arriving at the answer.

Research by neurobiologist Sian Beilock (Beilock, 2010) and others has revealed what they refer to as implicit memory that experts develop throughout their careers. This amounts to the accumulated wisdom built up from years of practice. When knowledge becomes this well learned, it becomes automated— less conscious—which is why we function so well at that stage of expertise. The problem is, if we want our students to even begin to learn that implicit knowledge, we may not be aware enough of it to share it with them. Here is my personal experience with this challenge: years ago I used to teach social, partner dancing in the evenings. I was asked by a dance friend to begin co-teaching her dance class with her. At that time I had spent maybe three years learning how to dance various social dance forms. That process involved watching my own instructors move in certain ways, try to copy their movements and leads, practice them over and over until I no longer was burdened by the necessity of consciously thinking of them as a series of successive steps. My instructors would talk about "muscle memory" in this regard and I could recognize my own progress as a dancer when my movements became fluid and I had the available consciousness to even add little embellishments of my own. Musicians and sport professionals experience this learning phenomenon. However, when my friend turned the tables on me by asking me to start teaching dance with her, I realized I now had the task of extricating all that muscle memory and bringing it back into my consciousness in order to teach it to others. I've heard dance instructors say beginning dancers have huge heads and tiny bodies, whereas experienced dancers have tiny heads and huge bodies. Dance teachers, therefore, must have huge heads *and* huge bodies.

These examples raise a critical issue in reflective teaching: it takes time. In fact, reflection in any context takes time. Over my lifetime I have been struck by what seems like an acceleration in the speed with which individuals process their daily tasks and experiences—including teachers—leaving little, if any time to stop, move back and reflect on what they are doing and look at the big picture. I hear news blurbs on the radio driving into work that young people today rarely, if ever, think down the road even five years as to the trajectory of their lives. I don't believe society has always been like this, that we are capable of slowing our pace periodically in order to better manage our functionality and direction. Even more than parents, I believe teachers have the responsibility to model the value and benefit of good reflectivity with their students.

So, back to the challenge of effectively fitting reflection into our busy daily routines. What I suggest to my students is something I mentioned earlier: keeping a teaching journal. I have been encouraged when I hear from some of my students they have kept journals. However, those that do are in the minority. If so far in this chapter I have succeeded in convincing you of the value of reflection and keeping a journal of your reflections, how can you fit the time required into your day to regularly make entries in it? For those who currently do not journal, do you spend any time on a regular basis to keep yourself in reasonable physical shape? Do you jog, ride a bike, take walks, walk your pet? If you do any of those things you have succeeded in carving out of your regular routine blocks of time anywhere between a quarter of an hour to an hour. When we think of journaling, we may have an image of jotting words down in a notebook or pad. However, with today's technology, all you need is a smartphone. Imagine taking a walk in the woods, either alone, or with your dog and reflecting back on the day's happenings (something you probably already do—but make no records of): your office hour meetings with students, your experiences grading your students' papers, your thoughts on how to facilitate the next class discussion, what visuals to improve your last PowerPoint presentation. All you have to do is use the audio or video recorder on your smart phone to record your thoughts on these matters while you are using your precious time doing something you had already become committed to. The next step would be to review your records each week and use them to recognize patterns, like how different you may sound at the beginning of the week from the end of the week; how you react to different people and situations without being aware of it; set goals; articulate ideas; revise approaches to certain problems; invent new principles of teaching. The longer you maintain a journal, the broader the database of mineable information to continually develop and become more efficient. Being more efficient implies saving time, and wasn't the cost of time required the primary argument you originally made to avoid keeping a journal?

If you're still not convinced, create your own empirical experiment: make the commitment to keep a journal for one week, analyze your records and see what you come up with. If it feels like you're doing it just for the sake of doing it, you're not doing it right. Remember, these are notes to help yourself. If what you've written/recorded isn't useful, you're not focusing on the right things. A journal, in my mind, is not a diary. It is not a record of merely what happened, but an analysis of why certain things may have happened as they did; it is about problem solving—for any experience you recall, if you had it to do over again, what might you do differently? The best test for good journaling is that it be useful to you. If it hasn't been, try something different. At its most elementary level, it may simply begin as a cathartic discharge, but don't let it stop there. Timing is another important factor: we all can rank the events of a day or a week's interactions and experiences into a prioritized order, with the most significant and critical at the top of our list. Those are the items worth reflecting on in more depth. Don't let too much time go by before addressing them or important details may become lost to memory. Part of what you can be doing is rewriting scripts of failed interactions. Even though those interactions are past you are building a toolbox of new approaches, responses—and as we have said—*principles* to guide you more successfully in the future.

Chapter 2 Principles:

1. Make records of your teaching experiences regularly by reflecting on what worked, what didn't and what you'd do differently if you had it to do over again. This activity can help generate and refine principles to guide your teaching.
2. When making decisions about the use of technology in teaching, fit the method/technology to your clearly articulated and refined learning outcomes.
3. Devise ways to deliver content before/outside of class so that class time can be used to interactively determine to what degree students are integrating it.
4. Build periodic interactive exercises into PowerPoint presentations.

References

Argyris, C. & Schon, D. *Theory in Practice: Increasing Professional Effectiveness.* San Francisco: Jossey-Bass, 1974.

Schön, D. (1983) *The Reflective Practitioner – How Professionals Think in Action.* New York, Basic Books.

Brookfield, S. (1995). *Becoming a critically reflective teacher.* San Francisco, CA: Jossey-Bass.

Perry, W (1970) *Forms of Intellectual and Ethical Development in the College Years,* Holt Reinhart/Jossey-Bass

Asato, M.R., Terwilliger, R., Woo, J. and Luna, B. White matter development in adolescence: a DTI study. Cereb Cortex. 2010 Sep;20(9): 2122-31. Epub 2010 Jan 5.

Huston, T. (2009). *Teaching What You Don't Know.* Cambridge, MA. Harvard University Press.

June 1980 (Carnegie Mellon University -- Complex Information Processing (CIP) -- Paper #410 -- "Expert and Novice Performance in Solving Physics Problems" -- Larkin, McDermott, Simon and Simon -- 1979-1980) [http://digitalcollections.library.cmu.edu/portal/main.jsp?flag=browse&smd=1&awdid=1]

Beilock, S. (2010). *Choke – What the secrets of the brain reveal about getting it right when you have to.* New York. Free Press.

Chapter 3
The Role of Higher Education in Society

What role does higher education play in society? Has it changed over time? What is different between the role of education in general to society and that of higher education? These are not only intriguing questions but important focal points for reflection by teachers everywhere. Beginning teachers may be more focused on questions having to do with *how* to teach. These questions bring our focus more on to *what* we should be teaching.

To begin answering these questions, a bit of historical inquiry can be helpful. A longer historical view of the purpose, structure and practice of teaching in higher education can be revealed by looking into the history of the university. How do the origins of both the structure and role of universities still influence their structure and role in society today? To what degree are the educational institutions of higher education adaptable to the changing needs of society? We certainly know they are adaptable to the economic changes within society because those institutions that weren't no longer exist. But for those higher educational institutions that exist in today's world, how sustainable are they in their current forms?

Any one who aspires and succeeds in becoming a faculty member in higher education will find their role as a member of the academic community expand over time. In the beginning they may focus on balancing the demands of teaching and research and getting tenure. At this point they may either seek or be assigned a faculty mentor. As time goes on, the role of service to their department, their college and institution will call to them with broader demands like curricular and program reviews, departmental politics around staffing and hiring and promotion responsibilities. After tenure they may be asked or choose to mentor newly hired faculty colleagues. They may be asked or choose to serve on institutional committees dealing with issues like accreditation, diversity or public service. Then there is their choice of how to serve reasonably and effectively within their discipline. All of these career milestones will require the faculty member to draw upon an evolving sense of the function and purposes of higher education within an ever changing world.

So, let's take a trip back in time. You may recall the image of the Alexandrian "lecture hall" included in Chapter 1. I call it a lecture hall because to me that's what it looks like—it looks very familiar. Compare that image to the one above [http://media. designerpages.com/3rings/2011/10/07/vycom-lecture-halls-by-nevins/] of a modern lecture hall designed around the business school practice of case-based teaching. We see the same tiered, circular seating with a lectern centrally located. This arrangement was designed to allow the instructor to interact more closely to individual students during case analyses. So lecturing may not have been what was transpiring between teachers and students in that Alexandrian space. Reviewing the Socratic dialogues recounted by Plato around the same time we see interactivity defined what was happening between teacher and students—there were dialogues between people. These dialogues had an influence and connection with regular daily dialogues the students had with friends, family and those they worked with outside of their educational experiences. One definition of educate is "to give intellectual, moral and social instruction to someone." This sounds a lot like parenting. From those early days of the Greeks what was called *artes liberales*, or liberal arts formed the basis of the ideal education, the purpose of which was to prepare men (women were not included in these early days of formal education) to "free the soul by drawing it up out of the material and transient world towards the ideal heights of pure knowledge." (Pedersen, 1997, p. 23). The curriculum evolved to include grammar, rhetoric, dialectic, geometry, arithmetic, astronomy, music, medicine and architecture, although the latter two areas of medicine and architecture were eventually dropped from this curricular list.

This classical form of education formed the basis of early American higher education in its first universities and colleges. In his book, *Our Underachieving Colleges: A Candid Look at How Much Students Learn and Why They Should Be Learning More*, Derek Bok (Bok, 2006) refers to an 1828 report from Yale College, "which held that the principle aim of college instruction was not to supply all of the important information that students may someday use but to instill mental discipline." (Bok, 2006, p. 13). However, not even the earliest higher education institution in England—Oxford—could insure that its students would learn discipline as recounted by Benjamin Franklin in Chapter Six of his Autobiography:

> It was an odd thing to find an Oxford scholar in the situation of a bought servant. He was not more than eighteen years of age, and gave me this account of himself; that he was born in Gloucester, educated at a grammar-school there, had been distinguish'd among the scholars for some apparent superiority in performing his part, when they exhibited plays; belong'd to the Witty Club there, and had written some pieces in prose and verse, which were printed in the Gloucester newspapers; thence he was sent to Oxford; where he

continued about a year, but not well satisfi'd, wishing of all things to see London, and become a player.

At length, receiving his quarterly allowance of fifteen guineas, instead of discharging his debts he walk'd out of town, hid his gown in a furze bush, and footed it to London, where, having no friend to advise him, he fell into bad company, soon spent his guineas, found no means of being introduc'd among the players, grew necessitous, pawn'd his cloaths, and wanted bread. Walking the street very hungry, and not knowing what to do with himself, a crimp's bill was put into his hand, offering immediate entertainment and encouragement to such as would bind themselves to serve in America.

He went directly, sign'd the indentures, was put into the ship, and came over, never writing a line to acquaint his friends what was become of him. He was lively, witty, good-natur'd, and a pleasant companion, but idle, thoughtless, and imprudent to the last degree.

No parent with a college age son or daughter would want such an outcome after investing in their higher education experience. So, what should a college education consist of? Bok goes on to note that Edward Thorndike's work in the early 20th century suggested "that the skills acquired through painstaking translations of Cicero and Virgil would rarely help students to analyze and solve problems outside the realm of Latin texts." (Bok, p. 13). Cornell's first president, Andrew Dickson White, also supported moving away from a strict classical curriculum: "The attempt to give mental discipline by studies which the mind does not desire is as unwise as to attempt to give physical nourishment by food which the body does not desire. . . . Vigorous, energetic study, prompted by enthusiasm or a high sense of the value of the subject, is the only kind of study not positively hurtful to mental power." (Bok quoting White, p. 15)

We see this conflict of the content and purpose of a higher education still playing out today in debates between colleges of arts and sciences in their defense of a liberal arts education and our professional and vocational schools. Bok laments that in the move, based on societal and economic pressures, away from the classical focus on moral and ethical reasoning and civic responsibility "two well-known educational goals with roots extending back to ancient Greece have been allowed to languish on most college campuses without much notice, let alone careful debate." (Bok, 2006, p. 42).

These questions of content and purpose of higher education may not be at the forefront of newly hired faculty members' attention, but over time, the relative place and societal contribution of their discipline will become a matter of serious consideration. Whether it is designing a course or planning an individual class, where do life-long, general skills and attitudes fit in with the content-specific substance to be taught? Accrediting agencies looking at an institution's added value to its students' lives during their four years of attendance look at learning outcomes and how they are assessed, among other things. Considering the cost of a higher education, both parents and their college-bound children can reasonably expect the experience can prepare them to adequately function in society. Life-long skills like the ability to communicate orally and in written form, think critically, be tolerant of different opinions, work collaboratively with a diverse group of people, be able to find and evaluate necessary sources of information, commit to learning throughout their lives—where do these outcomes fit in to a course in genetics? Hotel Administration? Veterinary medicine? Physics?

The Carnegie Foundation for the Advancement of Teaching was founded in 1905 "to [develop] networks of ideas, individuals, and institutions to advance teaching and learning. We join together scholars, practitioners, and designers in new ways to solve problems of educational practice." Ernest Boyer, one of the presidents of the Carnegie Foundation from 1979 to his death in 1995, developed a framework for the role of higher education in American society he called "The Scholarship of Engagement" (Boyer, 1996; http://www.compact.org/wp-content/uploads/2009/05/boyer-1996.pdf). At the time it was published posthumously in 1996, he pointed out that public confidence in the promise of higher education had waned from the growth spurt it had experienced after the second world war, stimulated by the GI Bill. In contrast to the country's collective commitment dealing with a global war, he recognized no equivalent current "urgent national endeavor" seemed to exist at that time. His call for a scholarship of engagement between higher education and society was a call to fulfill its potential for finding answers to world problems.

Such a calling was in contrast to the established structure of academia—based on academic disciplines whose potential knowledge had been siloed into college-based departments. When we look at the world today, global conflict still exists, but is scattered around the world in attacks on failed and failing governments by terrorist organizations. Beyond this is the continual threat to all societies by environmental and ecological degradation to the point where one major concern is how to feed the ever-growing human population while soil and water quality are increasingly threatened. Governments are increasingly discordant both within themselves and between countries. What Boyer was referring to as an urgent national endeavor has become an urgent global endeavor. As Boyer points out the historical contributions of higher education in his lifetime, in today's world, the potential for higher education's contributions to addressing world problems is threatened by economics. Students are now graduating with the burdens of large student debt. The job market has shifted to a more service- and technology-oriented economy. Available jobs are more competitive for graduating students to qualify for. In certain humanities disciplines, academic positions are very hard to come by. The pace of inflation for the cost of a higher education is not sustainable.

Boyer was calling for individual academics to extend their engagement beyond their professional disciplines and institutions to the problems of society at large. That was almost 20 years ago. To what degree has higher education responded to this calling? It is clear that it has in some aspects. Divisions between disciplines are becoming more permeable. Engineers are collaborating with biologists. Universities are establishing campuses in foreign countries and establishing more formal global networks. But there remain some issues of concern: so long as job security for faculty members—particularly at large research universities—is based on a tenure system that rewards research at the expense of teaching, that fills libraries and databases with more and more published information (due to the publish-or-perish mandate) for scholars to sift through for productive relative value, that puts faculty members in competition with each other through a bankrupt system for evaluating and rewarding good teaching, that in fact, focuses more on teaching than on student learning and has not encompassed a commitment to expanding disciplined research on how students learn within each academic field—we have a long ways to go yet. Since Boyer's piece, Lee Shulman, who succeeded Boyer as President of the Carnegie Foundation has called for a scholarship of teaching. Now he's talking about doing scholarship on one's own teaching and publishing the results for public review, critique and discussion. For busy academics, that may be a tall order.

What these efforts by Boyer and Shulman suggest to current practicing academics is go beyond the parochial research in your fields by putting effort into integrating it into society and connecting its relative contribution to addressing world problems. They're reminding academics they have a responsibility to share their growing knowledge in meaningful ways with citizens at large—to heighten the average non-academic's appreciation and value of higher education. The attitude of anti-intellectualism that has persisted beyond Richard Hofstadter's work in the 1960s (Hofstadter, 1963) has remained for many citizens because of a sense of alienation from academics and in some cases even condescension by them. There are, however, signs that academics are, in fact, reaching out to communicate with society at large through efforts like Neal deGrasse Tyson and his television homage to Carl Sagan: *Cosmos: A Spacetime Odyssey*; Brian Greene and his courageous effort to make quantum and string theories accessible to the public through the PBS series *The Elegant Universe*, and other educational programming.

In fact, these recent efforts at engagements between academics and society through the medium of television have been with us for at least 50 years. Boyer refers to the work of Jacob Bronowski, a mathematician who wrote *Science and Human Values*, (Bronowski, 1965) a combination of three essays stimulated by his visit to Hiroshima at the end of the second world war. Bronowski became more known beyond academia by his PBS series, *The Ascent of Man* that appeared during the 1970s. In one episode titled, "Knowledge or Certainty" he passionately helps the viewer make connections between the inevitable reality of internal error in scientific measurement through an explanation of the Gaussian Curve, the nature and limitations in human knowledge, the proviciality of university towns where academics may tend to be cloistered from the world at large—where, as he says, "students come not to worship what is known, but to question it." He ends the program very dramatically by visiting the site of the concentration camp at Auschwitz, walking into a pool where the ashes of cremated members of his family were flushed saying, "I owe it as a human being to the members of my family who died here to stand here as a survivor and a witness." Reaching into the pool and bringing up a handful of mud and ash, he ends the episode by saying, "we have to touch people."

https://www.youtube.com/watch?v=wXwj4jMnWZg

Bronowski's presence in British culture, and elsewhere The Ascent of Man was broadcast can be partially measured by the fact that he was cited in a Monty Python sketch:

Exploding Penguin sketch:

Pepperpot 2: Perhaps it's from the zoo.

Pepperpot 1: Which zoo?

Pepperpot 2: How should I know which zoo? I'm not Dr. Bloody Bronowski!

Pepperpot 1: How does Dr. Bronowski know which zoo it came from?

Pepperpot 2: He knows everything.

Pepperpot 1: Ooh, I wouldn't like that. It'd take all the mystery out of life. Anyway, if it came from the zoo, it'd have 'Property of the Zoo' stamped on it.

In his Foreword to the 2011 edition of Bronowski's book edition of *The Ascent of Man*, Richard Dawkins apologizes for referring to him as a renaissance man. He then goes on to justify this reference since, throughout his life, Bronowski maintained his interest not only in science but in the arts:

> "...who more than Bronowski weaves a deep knowledge of history, art, cultural anthropology, literature and philosophy into one seamless cloth with his science?"

In today's world, beginning academics may not have been trained, or even be interested in such an integrated breadth of knowledge as Bronowski's education lead him to develop, but he is an exemplary case of the benefits of a classical, liberal arts education. In his Introduction to the print version of The Ascent of Man, Bronowski explains what compelled him to accept the BBC's invitation to create the series:

> Unlike a lecture or a cinema show, television is not directed at crowds. It is addressed to two or three people in a room, as a conversation face-to-face—a one-sided conversation for the most part, as the book is, but homely and Socratic nevertheless.

If Bronowski could see how some people relate to television

today, he might come to see that it is not always in a "conversational" context. In explaining his approach to the broad content of the series that bridged science, human history and art, Bronowski had this to say,

> There cannot be a philosophy, there cannot even be a decent science, without humanity. I hope that sense of affirmation is manifest in this book. For me, the understanding of nature has as its goal the understanding of human nature, and the human condition within nature.

In the reissue of his essays on Science and Human Values in book form, Bronowski added a last footnote indicating his most recent thinking about the relationship between science and art:

> In science and in the arts the sense of freedom which the creative man feels in his work derives from what I have earlier called the poetic element in it: the uninhibited activity of exploring the medium for its own sake, and discovering as if in play what can be done with it.

Bronowski's academic authority grew out of both his academic training at Cambridge and his unique identity that empowered him to see the connections between the sciences and the arts:

> There are two clear differences between a work of art and a scientific paper. One is that in the work of art the painter is visibly taking the world to pieces and putting it together on the same canvas. And the other is that you can watch him thinking while he is doing it. (For example, Georges Seurat putting one coloured dot beside another of a different colour to get the total effect in *Young Woman with a Powder Puff* and *Le Bec.*) In both those respects the scientific paper is often deficient. It often is only analytic; and it almost always hides the process of thought in its impersonal language.

It is sobering to consider whether the efforts of academics like Boyer, DeGrasse Tyson, Bronowsky and Greene at engaging with society beyond academia would have contributed to their having been granted tenure based in part on these television appearances. The issue these exemplars might raise for consideration by prospective academics is what drives you? What risks will you be willing to make in your career to remain true to your strongly held values? In Bronowski's case, the effort to produce the Ascent of Man series, where he traveled from places like Easter Island to Gottingen, Germany and the Greek island of Samos, may have contributed to his early death at the age of 66, for he passed away soon after the series appeared on the PBS network. To what degree was Bronowski motivated out of personal life experience or out of his classical liberal arts education? I'm sure it was both. Cornell University president at the time of this writing, David Skorton, is a cardiologist by training. After having served as president of two large research universities, the University of Iowa and Cornell, he has moved beyond academia to become the Director of the Smithsonian Institution. In the socialization that you've been exposed to in graduate school do you owe your allegiance to your department, discipline, institution? My definition of socialization is you are learning things—knowledge, skills and most importantly to this discussion, attitudes—that you are not aware of learning and that in some cases you would have preferred not to learn had you a more conscious choice. Someone right out of graduate school will not feel empowered to be very choosy when responding to economic forces in the academic job market, or after gaining employment as a new hire, become too vociferous in bucking faculty politics they don't agree with. But none of us want to experience the nightmare of waking up one day to ask ourselves questions like, "How did I get here? Why am I doing these things?"

Chapter 3 Principles

1. To help keep your academic career path true to your personal values, and to create meaningful learning experiences for your students that extend beyond your courses and their schooling, maintain a clear vision of your view of the role of higher education in our ever-evolving society.
2. Articulate for yourself and your students your personal view on the relationship between the sciences and humanities.

3. Periodically review your vision for your career as it unfolds to be clear of your potential audiences.

References

Bok, D. (2006). *Our underachieving colleges : A candid look at how much students learn and why they should be learning more.* Princeton, NJ. Princeton University Press.

Hofstadter, R. (1963). *Anti-intellectualism in American life.* New York: Knopf.

Bronowski, J. (1965). *Science and human values.* New York: Julian Messner.

Pedersen, O. (1997). *The first universities.* Cambridge, UK. Cambridge University Press.

Chapter 4
Preparing to Teach

One of the most critical skills in being a successful teacher is prep work. Time spent thinking clearly about your course and classes before you teach them will pay off incredibly once things get underway. Two important concepts relevant here are effectiveness and efficiency. Drawing on both my own personal experience and from working with hundreds of graduate teaching assistants and faculty members over the years, the tendency for those just beginning is to either under-prepare or over-prepare. Here are some examples: it is not sufficient to assign a reading, then walk into a class and begin by asking, "What did you think about the reading?" This sounds like a stupid way to begin, and it is, but it is not much different than what I've actually witnessed in many cases where the instructor begins with a general, unfocused question like, "What questions do you have about the readings?" So that is one example of being under-prepared. The danger of over-preparing looks quite different. I think what drives many instructors into over-preparing is the fear of loosing control—control of covering the planned material in the time allotted. It is interesting to consider the metaphor of "covering the material" teachers often talk about. What about *un*covering the material? Over-preparation can result in the teacher dominating most, if not all, class time—resulting in what? Learning? Meaningful retention of material? I doubt it.

So, how can teachers effectively and efficiently prepare for teaching their courses and classes? Prep work takes up much more time than the actual teaching of the prepared plan. In fact, the time spent actually teaching while in class is a relatively small percentage of the time required to teach. Therefore, teachers will want to make sure that the time they do spend preparing their courses and classes contributes to effective learning in their students as well as making sure the time they do spend is efficient—with all the other tasks at hand, no one wants to be wasting their time in preparatory activities that result in ephemeral learning.

Prep work has two dimensions: macro and micro. Macro is about course design—the global perspective of a course: objectives, teaching strategies, assessment methods, readings, use of technology, syllabus design. Micro refers to the process of designing an individual class within that course: how time will be spent, what teaching and learning strategies will be used, the relationship between what happens within class time and what students are expected to be doing in the course out of class. One cannot be very effective in planning a class without having a well designed plan for the overall course. This may seem obvious, but much of the problems I've witnessed in unsuccessful courses have to do with the instructor's insufficient macro prep. This chapter will review what have become best practices (Fink, 2003; Wiggins & McTighe, 2001) in both macro and micro prepping for teachers, drawing on the extensive and ever-growing literature in this area.

Effective Course Design

To liberate teachers from socialized practices they may have inadvertently picked up from observing others, I suggest they begin by thinking about their course as an experience. What kind of experience do they want their students to have in their course? Enlightening, awesome, stimulating, life-changing? or tiresome, frustrating, anxiety-ridden, irrelevant, boring? To help in this liberation process, I use an analogy. I once heard a speaker describe their frustration in teaching in terms of being on one side of a river and yelling across the flowing water to their students on the other bank and hoping they could hear them and grasp their message. That sounds a lot like lecturing. Let's extend this image to a more creative and effective process. Instead of being on the opposite shore from your students, imagine your teaching role as a river tour guide. Now you join your students—all together in the same boat—where the nature of the relationship has changed. Since you are all in the same boat, you are now in a *collaborative* process exploring the river of course material. You will be guiding the students during the journey on the river, but they will be working with you to make sure you all get to the desired destination. Imagine scenes like, "Up around the bend there, the water gets deeper and slows down. Therefore, we will be able to drop anchor and fish and look around for a while." or, "After we visit the deep water, we'll be in for some rapids, so we'll all have to work together to fend off from rocks and other dangerous obstacles. Is everybody on board with me on that?"

The single most common mistake I see teachers make in course design is to carve out too large a hunk of course content. This tendency deserves examination: why would anyone try to cover so much material in a course that they lose their students, frustrate and intimidate them and reinforce shallow memorization—especially when considering their own precious time, let alone that of their students? If we assume teachers' espoused theories intend their students meaningfully integrate new course material into what they already knew, unlearn any misconceptions they may have been holding at the start of the course, apply course material even beyond what is covered in the course, why would they design an experience that results in the opposite? I believe this has to do with what I call *frame of reference* (there's another concept of teaching). Higher education faculty, for the most part, design and teach courses in subjects they have mastered. From their frame of reference, what may seem like a reasonable amount of course content will frequently overwhelm and stress their students if they are expected to master it in a course.

Eric Mazur, professor of physics at Harvard, wrote a book, *Peer Instruction*, based on his realization that traditional ways of teaching and assessing his students was bankrupt. In it he describes how to redesign courses and repurpose class time use that he has empirical evidence results in deep, lasting learning. Professor Mazur is not alone in these efforts. Nobel laureate Carl Wieman, another professor of physics has been conducting research in the teaching and learning of physics for several years now. His findings can be explored in his on-line blog: http://www.

science20.com/cwieman. Beyond the field of physics, many other faculty throughout higher education are exploring what has become known as *flipping the classroom* (Bretzmann, 2013). This approach draws on work in higher education teaching over the past 20 years in *active learning* (Beichner, et al., 2009).

How can this work inform effective course design? Back to our river tour guide metaphor and a course as an experience. All of us over our lifetimes have been conditioned to think of teaching and learning in certain ways. As young pre-school children, our learning curve is amazing over our first few years. We learn a language, how our body works, how to interact with others—all before we begin formal schooling. The experience of these first years as learners can sometimes be scary and surprising, but if you watch a young child you'll also see evidence of them having fun. Learning at this stage is not work. Sometimes it might be hard and there may be problems along the way, but my question is, what happens to our early experience of learning once we begin formal schooling? There are encouraging efforts currently underway to change elementary education to maintain children's original positive experiences with learning (http://nieer.org). It is imperative that we do this if they are to address the serious problems of the world they will inherit. Consider the past. Charles Dickens' novel *Nicholas Nickelby* introduces us to the teacher from hell, Wackford Squeers. Dickens was inspired in creating the character Smike both from his own early childhood experiences, but also based on an event at William Shaw's Academy in Yorkshire in the village of Bowes [http://www.independent.co.uk/travel/dickens-wrote--and-drank--here-1200845.html]. On April 13, 1822 George Ashton Taylor, 19 years old, died from the treatment he suffered there. Looking back at this travesty, we might react, "No way!" However, looking the world over, we know that young children are continually abused and injured today. So, our educational history and models include some very bankrupt forms. They continue in our collective consciousness. You'll see it expressed as mothers, who were themselves abused, yell and berate their children in the food store or shopping mall.

As teachers we have a serious responsibility to work on continuing the trends away from these vestiges of our educational past.

Much of the literature on effective course design draws on an engineering method called backwards design. If you design a bridge that is so long, made out of a certain material, designed to carry a certain amount of weight and traffic, you have to start by calculating the forces you expect the bridge can withstand before proceeding further. In the same way, *backwards course design* suggests that to create successful learning, we have to first specify in measurable terms the learning outcomes we intend our students to achieve. In other words, we begin at the end of the process and work backwards. This introduces a relatively new term: *learning outcomes*. The term may sound alien, but the concept is not. Over the years, educational literature has continually referred to *objectives*. When I was in graduate school they were referred to as "behavioral objectives" because if the teacher had an objective in mind for their students they had no behavioral evidence for, how would they be able to assess their relative impact on the student's learning. Of course the problem with behavioral objectives is that not all learning outcomes may be expressed in terms of changed behavior. So now we talk about learning outcomes—the outcomes of our collaborative efforts with our students in our courses. If we put what may seem like jargon aside for the moment and look at teacher's intentions, anyone who has taught knows that to gauge your impact, you have to know what you're looking for. So, for those uncomfortable with the term learning outcome, I suggest the phrase "what are you looking for"—that's where we start in effective course design. The power and logic of this approach will become clearer as we examine the course design process further.

As we discussed in an earlier chapter, not all course outcomes may be content-based: those centered around physics, romance studies, law or biology. A course does not exist in a vacuum, it is part of a larger curriculum. Your course may be a prerequisite for successive courses. You may not have the time to teach your students the prerequisites you establish for your course, like a certain level of writing ability or computational skill. So when writing course outcomes, you are establishing the broad *boundaries* of your course. This means you are not only addressing what your course covers, but what it *doesn't* cover. When crafting a list of course outcomes for inclusion in your syllabus, you will be looking at things in a broad brush perspective. It is not effective to list more than 7-8 outcomes as the broad outcomes of a course. This is where prep on the macro level connects with ultimate prep on the micro level. For each class, you will want to specify equally measurable outcomes that break down the more general course outcomes listed in the syllabus for each class.

Once you have a very clear picture of the content and focus of your course in terms of its outcomes, you can proceed to the next stage of backwards course design: what teaching and learning strategies do you believe will likely contribute to your students achieving your intended outcomes. If the first stage in this process can be understood as "knowing what you're looking for" this stage has to do with "how will you get there." Back to the river tour guide analogy: as the content expert, your students who are in the boat with you can rely on you to know the territory you are all traversing. When you consider the content topography, you will know what places in the journey to stop and explore, and how much time each of them reasonably requires to do them justice. You will also know what tools to bring along to make that topography accessible to their relative frame of reference. This is where you will make critical decisions about how to invest the limited classroom time you have. As we have explored so far, if you don't have a clear picture of the outcomes you intend, you can expend much wasted time and effort with negligible results. As I have said earlier, many faculty members make the mistake of relying on the latest technological innovation to achieve their purposes. The problem with new innovations is early adopters are the pioneers willing to take the risks working the bugs out of them. But many years of having been a techno-geek has taught me there is a whole world of other teaching methods available to explore beyond a quick fix of technology, most with a stronger history and track record. Things that come to mind include role-playing, debates, the problem-based learning most medical and veterinary schools have adopted, simulations and even simple games. I recently observed a class in natural resources where the teacher adapted the board game monopoly to helping his students learn how to run a farm. He called it "Cropopoly."

The last stage of course design is making decisions to capture the valid evidence necessary to assess to what degree your students achieved the learning outcomes you set for them. Following the logic we've been building on: once you know what you're looking for, have determined what teaching and learning strategies are likely to help them achieve those outcomes, how will you know they have adequately achieved them? Having appropriate *evidence* is the key idea here. Introductory and survey courses are usually structured for breadth at the cost of depth. If the desired outcome is for students to have become familiar with a broad range of material, giving them tests on their retention of that material may provide sufficient evidence. However, for an upper-level course design to focus on depth over breadth, evidence of sufficient learning must take a different form, like papers, experiments and projects. If non-content outcomes like ethical reasoning or tolerance for contrasting points of view are part of the course design, then assessments like debates or role-plays may provide the necessary evidence.

Effective Class Design

On the micro level of teaching preparation is the challenge of creating effective classroom learning experiences. As we've emphasized earlier, effectiveness and efficiency are key to success at this level as well. Given that the goal of our efforts in the classroom is to impact our students' learning, the same backwards design process is equally relevant in planning individual classes as it is for planning courses. At the individual class level we become much more focused and specific from where we started on the macro level. Whereas a syllabus may contain less than 10 learning outcomes, when you add up all a course's classes over a term, there will be many more outcomes on that level, permitting the teacher to explore the subject in detail. For each class, depending on the teacher's planned outcomes, a variety of strategies will be employed to fit those specific outcomes. Assessment is also necessary on a micro class level as well since the teacher will need feedback from students to determine if their strategies are working and will want their students to experience a regular class-based sense of their relative grasping of the material. I want to emphasize, again, that just as on the macro level the teacher is creating an experience for their students, they are also creating learning experiences on a micro or class level. What kind of experience will work?

The most commonly used teaching strategies I've observed over the years are lecturing and the use of PowerPoint to deliver course content in class. But as the work of Mazur and Wieman have indicated, using class time to deliver course content is not very efficient in terms of lasting, deep learning. Some will argue that if there is no appropriate text, the instructor may be forced to cover the material through lecturing. But here is where new uses of technology can actually come to the aide in this situation: in the work on flipping the classroom teachers are using the new cameras built into their laptops and other recording devices to record their lectures and making the recordings available to their students before class so they can use class time to reinforce that material through in-class activities, or engage with their students to clear up misunderstandings or misconceptions. This practice is based on the recognition that learning takes time and just because students have been exposed to new material is no guarantee they have meaningfully and accurately integrated it. To truly integrate it requires them to interact with it in order to reinforce the new neural networks developing in their brains. Wieman cautions it takes thousands of hours to develop true expertise in an area. Anyone relying solely on lecturing may be fooling themselves they are employing an effective and efficient use of theirs and their students' time in class.

So why is lecturing still so prevalent in higher education? First of all, I'm not saying one should never lecture. Some of the most effective and inspiring teaching I've witnessed has been in lecture classes. I'm reminded of a time several years ago when I was invited to sit in on a lecture given by historian Walter LaFeber at Cornell. There were probably 250 students in the room. He walked in with little or no notes, began speaking and succeeded in capturing the room's attention throughout the 50 minutes of the class. Later I asked him how he prepared of his classes and he said he writes out his lecture in longhand and memorizes it. Some academics may still rely on this method for preparing their teaching, but I'm sure not everyone would be inclined to adopt it today. What made Professor LaFeber's lecture so captivating was the fact that the script he had written was a story—not surprising given he is an historian. If we think about how ubiquitous stories are in our lives, from our earliest childhood experiences, we can recognize their structure has been imprinted into our neural networks for most of our lives. This is what makes them so easy to capture our attention. This was brought to my attention by another Cornell professor of theatre who introduced me to what she called the dramatic arc. Anyone who has spent time watching television or attending movies has been programmed to respond to the dramatic arc. Script writers understand this and all the money invested in television programs and in producing movies is dependent upon the writer's ability to create a script that holds our attention for anywhere from short cartoons and music videos to multiple-hour long movies.

For those teachers wanting to create lecture scripts that capitalize on this notion of the dramatic arc, it will help to examine its structure. Stories have distinct parts: in their most simple form, they have a beginning, middle and end. What holds our attention in the dramatic arc is the continual series of challenges, impediments, failures that the story's protagonist runs up against and must overcome. This is very obvious in mysteries. We can see this effect in the works of Conan Doyle as well as in Charles Dickens. This is all very familiar to us and we get hooked into these stories easily due to the familiarity of this structure. But if we contrast this art of the dramatic arc with academic lecture scripts that are not based on stories but on covering a certain amount of technical content within a certain time, we begin to see why it is so easy for students' attentions to start drifting after only ten or fifteen minutes. This can be illustrated in the diagram below:

The black line represents the dramatic arc where the protagonist in our story has a task to perform, hits a problem they must overcome, succeeds, only to run into several more challenges before they reach the story's climax at the top, and then what follows in the end of the script is the resolution and denouement of the story. Imposed on that is a lighter, grey line that represents the results of some research that has been carried out looking at students' attention over a 50 minute class (Johnstone & Percival, 1976; Bligh, 2000). In that lighter, grey line we see they begin high in attention, but slowly start drifting away from the subject over time until they bottom out around 40-45 minutes. What is interesting is that, all things being equal: the instructor, subject, room, etc., their attention naturally starts to pick up within the last 10 minutes of the class. This diagram also shows how our story-based programming puts the climax at, or around, the same time as we would otherwise have bottomed out in our attention, and thus retention of the class material. So, the lesson here is, if you are writing lecture scripts, including the use of PowerPoint slides, and want to avoid the 40 minute slump, write your script structured on the dramatic arc.

Teachers today are struggling for their students' attention in competition with all their digital devices they are privileged to bring with them to class. This makes it even more imperative that we write effective class scripts to avoid wasting everyone's precious (and ever-more costly) time. One of Cornell's well-known professors, James Maas, taught introductory psychology for 40 years to classes that grew to over 1500 freshmen. I sat in on several of his classes over the years and could see he employed a method I call *varying the stimulus*. This means, being conscious of the reality that the average person's attention span starts to drift after 10-15 minutes, he would never employ any one method longer than that time limit—he would then vary the stimulus. If he had been lecturing for a while, he'd switch to a photograph or movie clip, then to a demonstration, then back to his PowerPoint slides. There are different ways of doing this. One has to do with varying the students' role from passive recipient to active engagement as in the use of clickers or the think-pair-share method. Yet another has to do with moving from the abstract to the concrete. Teachers who are now effectively using classroom response systems like "clickers" are able to break up the flow of passive content delivery with moments of active, cognitive reflection and integration through asking meaningful conceptual questions throughout the class. This form of varying the stimulus has multiple advantages: it can help keep the students alert paying attention if used properly, it provides the teacher with a means of assessing the class's relative level of understanding and it provides each student with a series of data points to recognize their own growing integration of the material.

An example of varying the stimulus between the abstract and concrete comes from Cornell engineering professor Charles Williamson who integrates demonstrations of abstract relationships and formulae into his classes through blowing giant smoke rings and launching wrapping paper tubes into the air and across the classroom. Each of these examples illustrates a different classroom experience. The instructor's skill has to do with devising a teaching and learning method they have determined can contribute to achieving the learning outcomes they set for their students in their classes. Several other Cornell engineering professors, Charles Seyler and Michael Kelley moved their class of 60+ students out of lecture halls to a lounge filled with tables so they could structure their students into groups at each table to use class time solving problems. Their script included the following instructions to the students, "Each one of you at your table is responsible for making sure that everyone else at your table can solve the problem." This freed them up to walk around and check in with each table to support the process, provide encouragement and direction, but not to solve the problems for the students. When I interviewed several of their students about this strategy, they said things like, it was fun, they were conscious of teaching each other which in turn helped them retain the material better, and they were making friends and forming relationships that extended beyond the class.

What I've tried to do in this chapter is show what is possible when teachers step out of unexamined methods of preparation for teaching that is primarily content-driven to approaching the task more like a movie script writer might when writing a captivating screen play. To do so is to be more process-driven—to use their experience as learners to craft experiences for their students that tap into the potential energy they bring to the situation. There is hope for those higher education teachers who lament that whenever they either stop periodically in class and ask, "Are there any questions?" or ask a more specific question, they are consistently rewarded in their efforts with dead silence and blank stares. To make the mistake of assuming today's students are not responsive does them an injustice. We will revisit the skill of creating effective learning experiences in more detail in the next chapter.

Principles to Chapter Four:

1. Backwards course design: follow these steps in this order:
2. What are you looking for in your students by the end of the course (what are your learning outcomes?)
3. How will you get there? (What teaching/learning methods and resources are likely to help you achieve your stated outcomes?)
4. How will you know you've gotten there? (What is your course assessment schema? What measurable evidence do you need to determine your learning outcomes' relative attainment?)
5. When designing your course, work from the learner's frame of reference and consider how you successfully learned the material, rather than being a slave to the content. This is called being process-driven.

References

Beichner, R. J., Saul, J. M., Abott, D. S., Morse, J. J., Deardorff, D. L., Allain, R. J., Bonham, S. W., Dancy, M. H., & Risley, J. S. (2007). The student-centered activities for large enrollment undergraduate programs (SCALE-UP) project. In E.F. Redish & P.J. Cooney (Eds.), *Research-based reform in university physics* (Vol. 1). College Park, MD: American Association of Physics Teachers. Retrieved October 12, 2009 from http://www.compadre.org/per/per_reviews/volume1.cfm.

Bligh, D.A. (2000). *What's the use of lectures.* San Francisco: Josses-Bass.

Johnstone, A. H., & Percival, F. (1976). Attention breaks in lectures, *Education in Chemistry, 13*(2), 49-50.

Chapter 5
Creating Effective Learning Experiences

This chapter addresses the challenges of how to use class time effectively. It builds on what has been said in the earlier chapter about preparing to teach. What we will explore in more detail encompasses both planning and execution of your teaching plans. The execution of a class teaching plan is a discrete skill from planning for that class. No teacher, regardless of his or her method of planning a class, whether by using technology like PowerPoint, role-playing, simulations or other teaching and learning strategies, ever carries out that plan exactly as scripted. This is because there are so many variables, they require the teacher to make what have been referred to as *decisions on the fly* in the classroom. In fact, a core skill in effective teaching has to do with making good decisions. Let's look at a couple of examples we're already familiar with.

You spend time putting together a teaching plan based on PowerPoint slides and then find when you deliver the presentation to your students, you end up reading much of what you've written on them which disengages your students. This points out a lack of good decisions regarding the effective use of PowerPoint. PowerPoint can be used to create effective learning experiences, but clearly, there are some basic do's and don'ts.

Now, let's assume we move the level of decision making to the decisions you make on the fly in the execution of a more effective teaching plan using PowerPoint. You have a planned question on a slide you want your students to think about and respond to, maybe through a think-pair-share. You reveal the question on a PowerPoint slide, give them a time limit to discuss their responses with a partner, and then pick on a pair to respond. Let's say in this case what you get is either wrong or something completely irrelevant. How do you respond at this point? The decision you make on the spot can have both a short-term and long-term effect not only with your relationship with those students, but in its effect on the general classroom atmosphere for the remainder of the course! How you respond in the moment draws on a completely different skill set than the skills you used to plan your slides and that question.

Over time, students' experiences in their relationship with you in class can be assessed through having them periodically fill out surveys to help you gauge how well you're doing in this skill. Traditionally, these surveys are administered at the end of a course, but it is more effective to ask students for their feedback on your teaching methods earlier in the course, particularly if you are experimenting with new teaching approaches. With all the time and effort teachers put into both planning for their classes and trying to execute their plans effectively, everyone wants these efforts to pay off in meaningful and sustained learning. How can we plan and interact with our students in class to achieve that deeper learning?

As mentioned in an earlier chapter, I have come to think about the time spent in class with my students as an *experience* based on a *script*. When making decisions to plan for that experience it helps me to visualize what kind of experience I'm trying to create. Naturally I want it to be engaging, stimulating, enlightening and fun. However, how many of us have left classes we've taken where we experience frustration, confusion, anxiety and diminished confidence? None of us want that in our classes so what are some principles that can assist us in avoiding these negative experiences and help us achieve the more productive and positive experiences?

To get a better sense of an effective learning experience, try this: reflect back over your life and bring to mind the most powerful learning experiences you've had. I'm sure they would include any of the following characteristics: transforming, sustained, emotionally charged, surprising, painful, empowering and fulfilling. I'll bet most of them happened in an environment other than a classroom. So, an effective learning experience is a kind of space—physical, emotional, psychological, intellectual and even spiritual. There is a vast and ever-growing body of research and literature about teaching methods that can contribute to effective learning experiences (Bonwell & Eison, 1991; Angelo & Cross, 1993; Weimer, 2002). We have reviewed some of its themes so far in earlier chapters: the work on active learning and engaging students.

Randy Olson (2009), who started his career as a marine biologist writes about his journey from academic to film maker in his book *Don't be such a scientist*. The thesis of his book is: first you have to arouse and motivate, only then can you fulfill your goals and educate. What motivated him to leave academia, move to Hollywood and go to film school grew out of years of going to national conferences where he would sit in the audiences with other marine biologists and suffer through horrendous presentations by the top names in the field. When he reflected on how effective TV and movie script writers were in getting and holding our attention, he made a commitment to learn how they do that. I described this in an earlier chapter when I explained the dramatic arc. So rather than constraining ourselves to writing a script for a class that is limited to technical information exchange and simply a roadmap of what *we* as the teacher have to do during the class, we must take into consideration *how people learn* in our planning and execution of our plans to have a lasting impact on our *students'* learning. No one will learn anything (other than maybe to drop your class) if you can't get their sustained attention and motivate them to follow your script. What separates academia from Hollywood is we are in the business of educating people, not merely entertaining them. We must be driven by our goals—and in the current language—learning outcomes. Our job is to create experiences that result in prolonged, sustainable learning. Let's look at some useful tools to draw upon in this endeavor: role-playing and simulations, both of which are being used effectively and more frequently in higher education.

I expect that most of you reading this may have had an experience with an educational simulation. If we unpack the basic components of that method, our inventory will include:

- drawing on prior knowledge and experience—which neurobiologists would say requires certain neuronal pathways we have developed to both fire and start extending as we apply them in new contexts
- collaborative learning as our students interact with each other
- competition and teamwork if we break our students into groups
- and even a bit of mystery regarding how the whole thing will work out.

In Randy Olson's terms we would be using a very arousing and motivating script.

Role-playing is a method even closer to what Olson suggests. The question is how to effectively use role-playing in your class and its subject matter. Some may be discouraged from turning to role-playing as a teaching and learning strategy because they may feel it isn't appropriate for what they're teaching. I once heard of a teacher who used role-playing to teach osmosis in a biology course. More recently a professor teaching a course on infectious diseases used a variation of role-playing called *reacting to the past* [https://reacting.barnard.edu] in his course. This happened not long after the terrible Haitian earthquake where a wide-spread cholera epidemic developed. The course instructors created a script based on the 1854 cholera epidemic in London to have the students play the roles of the characters who interacted in that time and scenario to explore the aspects of controlling an infectious disease. To make it seem even more real, he moved his class to an on-campus location that was characteristic of the London locations of that event:

http://ithacabuilds.com/category/current-projects/sage-chapel-cornell/

If we unpack the basic characteristics of that method we see it contains:

- active engagement requiring empathy and stretching outside of one's point of view
- political sensitivity
- a need for fact-finding
- tolerance for others' beliefs
- problem solving
- and critical thinking.

It would be difficult to disengage from a class like this. Of course the instructor would have to take into consideration students' comfort level with role-playing and think of ways to prep them for the experience. However, much of that can be accessed from those who developed this growing teaching method from the web site at Barnard College: https://reacting.barnard.edu. If you peruse that web site you'll see that a book has been written about the method titled *Minds on Fire—How Role-Immersion Games Transform College* (Carnes, 2014). What make role-playing and simulation games effective teaching and learning strategies is that they are both very familiar to the young students of today who have grown up engaging in these activities on a very regular basis. They therefore address Olson's requirements of arousal and motivation, and they fulfill the academic requirements of educating and sustained learning by the way they are being framed and used by the higher education faculty using them.

Some may be discouraged from experimenting with such approaches due to a perception of added time for preparation. It is true employing such strategies may mean added prep time, but I don't believe the time required has to be much more than any other strategy, if one is first developing a new course. However, creating effective learning experiences for our students is not limited to these dramatic approaches—although there are plenty of on-line resources for instructors to avail themselves of for them (just Google role playing and/or educational simulations).

Let's look at a typical 50-minute class you might have to plan for and apply a simple strategy we're all familiar with from Hollywood: the notion I call *varying the stimulus*.

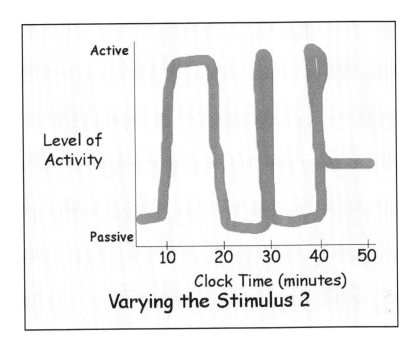

Varying the Stimulus 2

Here we're just thinking about the degree to which our script puts our students in a passive mode, like when we lecture, versus an active mode, as when we might employ an active learning strategy like a think-pair-share, or a clicker question. Thinking this way about our class as a learning experience capitalizes on what we know about average attention span, which is limited to 10-15 minutes. Generating a principle of teaching from this we might come up with: don't do anything for more than 10 minutes before varying the stimulus to something else. So if you've been talking for 10 minutes, move to asking a planned question, an activity, a video clip, an image, etc.

This concept of varying the stimulus can be thought of in other ways besides moving the students from a passive to an active role. Here's a second way to think about it to experiment with:

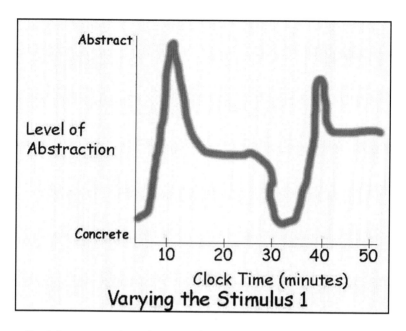

Varying the Stimulus 1

In this case we're also varying the stimulus for our students by moving from abstract to concrete after a time limit of around 10 minutes. Think about the familiar need to link theory with practice. An ineffective experience would be to dwell on the abstract theory from the instructor's relative comfort level for much of the class time, leaving many students wondering how it plays out in reality and frustrated for examples.

A very effective way of helping students connect abstract theory with concrete practice is to consider taking an inductive approach in your class script. In most cases I've observed, expert instructors who have integrated their comprehension of abstract theory will present that theory to their students and then hope or expect the students to deductively recognize where and how it plays out in reality. This presents a more challenging stretch to them than presenting an event or series of facts and then putting the students in the role of theorists to generate their own ways of theorizing. Regardless of how sound their reasoning or resultant theories may be, they are now more cognitively ready to understand formal theorists' explanations. We can take an example of this from entomology: a traditional way of teaching any taxonomic science like entomology or parasitology is to show a taxonomic system and then drill students to memorize where on the taxonomic system a specific species falls. Doing so reinforces lower level rote learning, which is what many instructors were introduced to when they were learning their relevant taxonomies. However, in some cases, like in parasitology, even experts find they have to regularly reclassify species from one year to another. Wouldn't it make more sense and be more fun to create a class learning experience whereby you turn the students into taxonomists and give them several species to classify and then discuss their relative logic behind their choices? Then when they are introduced to accepted taxonomic classifications the underlying theory might be more meaningful and therefore more memorable.

Research on learning by neurobiologists has recently revealed more effective ways to teach by creating different and more powerful learning experiences. Drawing examples from the book, *Make it stick*:

> Trying to solve a problem before being taught the solution leads to better learning, even when errors are made in the attempt (Brown, et al, 2014, p. 4)

Teaching problem solving traditionally involves modeling how to solve a problem in class, followed by some in-class practice by students—if there is time—and then assign them a problem set to practice further as homework. This approach may work with certain students, maybe the majority but what about those students where this approach doesn't work? Even for those students who receive high marks on their problem sets, how well have they learned what was intended? A neurobiological criticism of doing things this traditional way suggests that if you force students to struggle figuring out their own approaches, however ineffective, you are helping them build the necessary neurological pathways they can then build on when you as the expert help them fill in the gaps of their understanding. You have now helped your students extend those pathways to incorporate new neuronal firings, that when repeated through further practice and drill, will become more sustainable and available for retrieval from memory over time.

How can this play out in practice? I will share two examples from engineering. A professor of electrical engineering I've know for years used to teach his classes of 90+ students in the traditional lecture approach in lecture halls with fixed-row seating. He became frustrated that when he'd give them a problem to practice solving in that kind of classroom space, he couldn't get to all the students because the seats were in the way. So he moved his classes to a large lounge where they sat around tables in groups of six. Now he could add several other principles from what he knew about collaborative learning to the new class experience. At the beginning of the course he told the students that as they sat around their tables together, they were all responsible to make sure everyone else at their table could solve the problems they were assigned. Now they couldn't just work alone. I visited his class and made videos of the students working together and sure enough, they were teaching each other, while the instructors and graduate TAs walked around as resources who did not solve the problems for the students, but prompted them to help them figure them out by themselves.

I invited several of these students to my office to discuss how they experienced this approach. Here are some of the things they said:

> It was definitely fun . . . there are no stupid questions . . . when you bounce something off someone else, it's more hands-on and it makes it easier to remember and apply . . . If the facilitator just nudges me in the right direction, I can then figure it out for myself and feel good about myself in the end. . . . There's definitely a correlation between teaching each other and remembering the material better.

What's also significant about this approach is that it simulates how engineers work in the world outside of academia: they work collaboratively in teams.

My second example is from mechanical engineering where the instructor had also become frustrated with traditional ways of teaching and also changed the physical teaching and learning space. In this case he divided his class of about 50 students into sections of about 10-12 and had them all meet in a room with blackboards on three of the walls. They were then divided into pairs and all given challenging problems to solve with a partner. This freed him up to wander around between the pairs, listen to their ways of thinking about and solving the problem, asking them probing questions, prompting them when they were on the right track, but not solving the problems for them.

These examples illuminate different kinds of classroom experiences. In each case students were actively engaged, they couldn't fall asleep or be tempted to absent themselves through their digital devices. They experienced the approaches positively and had fun. There was no indication of boredom. There may have been moments of frustration, but those may have been followed up quickly by feelings of accomplishment and growing confidence, or at least by a sense of support from the instructor. Again, the neurobiologists have found this to be true through their research:

> people who are taught that learning is a struggle, that often involves making errors will go on to exhibit a greater propensity to tackle tough challenges and will tend to see mistakes not as failures, but as lessons and turning points along the path to mastery. (Brown, et al. p. 91)

From these examples and research insights, the reader may want to think about developing a system for designing effective classroom learning experiences. The important thing to keep in mind is to get a return on the investment of time and effort both for the instructor in planning and execution, as well as for the students and their efforts and challenges, otherwise those efforts and investments have been wasted.

When planning a class experience I find it helpful to think in terms of phases. The first phase is the warm up phase as was introduced in an earlier chapter. Warming up is more about making connections than about instruction. In Olson's terms you first have to arouse and motivate. Then the next and probably longest phase of your script is your choice of teaching and learning strategies. Besides simulations and role-playing as we've discussed earlier are laboratory activities, field trips, demonstrations, responding to video clips, which can stimulate emotional responses where required, debates, student presentations, competitions and a whole range of other creative ways to engage students and their growing neuronal pathways.

Let's look at another commonly used teaching and learning classroom strategy: discussions. In my experience working with both new and experienced teachers, creating effective discussions where students leave with outcomes they retain frequently proves to be a challenge. What often prevents success is the tendency for the instructor to dominate; students are shy to contribute because of concerns of being judged not just by the instructor, but more so by their peers and dominant students not self-monitoring enough to recognize when they need to make space for other voices. Building trust is a critical task for the instructor. Trust takes time to establish itself. The enemy of classroom trust is judgement. This can be illustrated by considering two potential responses by an instructor to when a student may say something either wrong, confusing or irrelevant in a discussion: "Yes but . . ." versus "If then . . ." When monitoring or facilitating a classroom discussion a critical concept of teaching is what I have referred to as *frame of reference*: the need to continually consider how responses to students might be experienced by them and affect their performance. If I respond to a student with a response like "Yes but . . ." the chances are I will shut that student down and discourage their continued participation. Alternatively, if I was to respond to a confusing or seemingly irrelevant comment by a student with something like, "That's interesting, tell me more about that?" I'm more likely to keep that student engaged and at the same time get added information about their thinking to either redirect them or to take corrective measures.

In my experience, discussions can be broken down into three phases: initiating, maintenance and closure. The instructor's role changes as these three phases evolve. The initiating phase requires more active participation by the instructor to overcome inertia, warm everyone up, get them connected to prior knowledge they bring to the conversation and focus everyone on the topic and task. If the instructor has been successful at initiating the discussion, the first indication the discussion has moved to the next phase is when a student responds to another student for the first time. If the instructor remains too dominant after the first phase, the discussion may remain in what I call the ping-pong pattern. This is where every student directs their comments back to the instructor, thus reinforcing him or her to verbally respond back every time. So, during the middle or maintenance phase, the instructor must play a more passive role and let the students run with the ball. If they carry it out of bounds, the instructor can step in and help maintain focus. If arguments get too personal they can act as referee by applying appropriate rules of engagement. If students' misconceptions threaten to derail the topic, the instructor can step in with corrective comments. All of these maintenance measures must be short. Eye contact is another important tool for the instructor during maintenance. Avoiding eye contact when students keep directing their comments to them can encourage the speaker to look elsewhere for a response.

This brings us to the last phase of a discussion, and for that matter, any class: that of closure. In a good discussion, participants become immersed in the conversation, responding to each other back and forth with responses and counter arguments and points of view. During this middle phase, they probably won't have the presence of mind to be taking notes or thinking about take-a-ways. An important skill for the instructor/facilitator in preparation for closure is what I call *discussion tracking*. As we have discussed, discussion, like lecturing, is simply one teaching/learning strategy. You choose a discussion to achieve certain outcomes for the class. The initiating questions to get things started, as well as the choice of topic are there for a reason. It would be a waste of everyone's time and energy if all that participants experienced at the end of a discussion class was that they had a good discussion but have no sense of what they got out of it. It is the instructor's responsibility to ensure that both during the maintenance phase and especially at the closure phase of class discussions students leave with relevant and appropriate take-a-ways they have integrated into their cognitive structures. To ensure this happens the instructor now plays a more active role in the last 5-10 minutes of the class to take the notes they wrote in their discussion tracking efforts and review the thrust and trajectory of the discussion in a summary. I recommend they do this in writing on the board, which will cue the students to take notes they will carry with them after the class is over.

What often happens, though, is due to poor time management, the instructor may not have time to do the closure and simply let the clock run out with no reinforcement of what the discussion has achieved. Therefore, an effectively facilitated discussion experience requires the instructor to budget time for the closure and step in at the necessary time to redirect the conversation. Whether the teaching/learning strategy is a discussion, lecture or field trip, the closure of the class is necessary to stimulate the students to integrate and consolidate in their brains all that has transpired in the class. After simulations or role-playing, a 5-10 minute period (or longer if necessary) at the end for debriefing will be required for students to reflect, make connections and make records of what they take with them from the experience. Creating scripts that can achieve this will help motivate students to participate in all your classes with the experience they know their efforts and participation will be intrinsically valuable.

Principles from Chapter 5

1. Solicit feedback from your students on teaching strategies early in the course so you can make adjustments that can improve how things are working and to engage with your students while they remain stakeholders in your course.
2. Don't use the same teaching/learning strategy in class for more than 10 minutes in order to vary the learning stimulus and maintain your students' attention.
3. When teaching problem solving, ask students to try to solve it first before instruction and only after they've given it a try model the solution to help them fill in the gaps of their understanding.
4. It can be more effective to teach theory by asking students to inductively generate theory from observation and factual data than by starting by teaching the theory and then asking them to apply it.
5. It helps to think of the phases of a class when planning a teaching/learning script: warm-up/initiating, maintenance and finally closure.

6. Avoid judgement in responding to student input during classroom interactions with students. Instead, ask for their reasoning in making a response to questionable comments.

7. Use discussion tracking to keep notes during student discussions to help summarize and emphasize main points at the end of the class to encourage note-taking of the take-a-ways. Write these points on the board in real time to cue students to write them in their own notes.

References

Angelo, T. A., & Cross, K. P. (1993). *Classroom assessment techniques* (2nd ed.). San Francisco: Jossey-Bass

Bonwell, C., & Eison, J. (1991) *Active learning: Creating excitement in the classroom*, Washington, DC: ASHE-ERIC.

Brown, P.C., Roediger III, H.L., & McDaniel, M.A. (2014). *Make it stick – The science of successful learning*. Cambridge, MA: Harvard University Press.

Carnes, M. (2014). *Minds on fire: How role-immersion games transform college*. Cambridge, MA. Harvard University Press.

Olson, R. (2009). *Don't be such a scientist*. Washington, DC: Island Press.

Weimer, M. (2002).*Learner-centered teaching: Five key changes to practice*. San Francisco: Jossey-Bass.

Chapter 6

Assessing Student Learning and Providing Effective Feedback

The title of this chapter implies the two primary areas of responsibility teachers have regarding their students' academic performance: formative and summative evaluation. Before we go into the distinction of these responsibilities and the work associated with them, it will be helpful to understand the distinction between assessment and evaluation. Of the many scholarly articles and books on the subject (Angelo & Cross, 1993; Huba & Freed, 2000; Suskie, 2009; Walvoord & Anderson, 2009), the primary difference between their use of the terms assessment vs. evaluation has to do with frequency. Whereas assessing something is an on-going activity over time, an evaluation happens once as a final measure of impact. To avoid confusing the reader who may come across these terms both in the literature and in discussions with academics, I will confine this discussion to the use of two other traditionally used terms encompassed in the title of this chapter: summative and formative.

All teachers need regular feedback and evidence from every one of their students as they interact together through an academic experience like a course in order to guide both the student in their learning and to guide themselves as instructors. This requirement for regular, on-going feedback is what formative assessment is all about. Formative assessment must be carried out both on a macro level over the course of an entire semester or term as well as on a micro level within each class meeting of that course. This micro-level has been referred to as classroom assessment (Angelo & Cross, 1993).

In contrast to formative assessment is summative assessment, referred to by some authors as evaluation. As the word summative implies, this is a process carried out at the end of an educative event like an academic course that produces a final measurement of the outcomes of that event. So, going back to the language I've used in this chapter's title, assessing your students' learning at the end of a course that produces their grade is summative assessment, whereas the comments, verbal discussions during office hours and e-mail exchanges you have with each of your students to guide their learning and further performances throughout your course is formative assessment. All instructors must do both. There are, as we've all experienced, potential pitfalls in doing either effectively. One pitfall has to do with the issue of subjectivity. Another has to do with timing and frequency.

Let's start by imagining a learning situation where there is no teacher, where the learner is being self-guided or regulated in their evolving performance. A good example might be learning a computer game. Regardless of the particulars of the game, the user has both on-going feedback and end-of-game performance rating, or scoring. If you're playing a game you are continually modifying your game play based on past performance and usually improving it, so over time, you can see an increase in your subsequent game scores. To become a master over time, you need both the formative feedback as well as the summative scores. This is something we all can relate to from personal experience, whether the game we're playing is computer-based or something like tennis.

Within an academic context, however, the stakes are higher. Our interactions with each of our students result in summative grades that go on their transcripts that have a major influence on their lives. We therefore are concerned with being fair, accurate, consistent and helpful. Common complaints of ineffective assessment practices include student comments like, "My grade doesn't accurately represent what I learned." or "I have no idea why I got this grade." From our perspective as instructors, we may have our own complaints: "I know this student is capable of better work, but for whatever reason, they're unable to give me evidence of their potential." or "What I'm getting from this student is suspiciously unauthentic."

Fortunately, there are some very important principles of assessment that can serve to guide the instructor in minimizing assessment problems. Notice I said "minimizing" not "eliminating." We can never eliminate all assessment problems for the same reason we can never arrive at the perfect teaching strategy: due to the innumerable variables involved. Let's start with the matter of objectivity. All teachers would like to think their assessment schemas are objective: that they are not being influenced by subjective bias one way or the other. The reality is you can never eliminate subjectivity; however, there are things you can do to minimize it. The first thing is to be consistent. One source of assessment bias is to let the identity of the individual student influence the standards or criteria one uses to grade them. This can be addressed in several ways. One way is through the use of a "blind" grading system, where the individual's identity is masked. That approach may work better in a standardized assessment, like a multiple-choice or true/false test. However, over time, as you get to know your students, you may be able to identify a student on writing samples like those contained in short answer and essay test questions.

If tests are a frequent assessment method, a necessary requirement before grading is to develop an answer/grading key in order to address another means of grading objectivity: being consistent. This is best done while writing the test questions. Consider the weighting and point value of each question first, then set the boundaries of a full-credit answer. This might involve a number of components in the student's answer, which will help in assigning the question's point value. Neurobiological research (Brown, et al, 2014) has supported the frequent use of testing as both a valid indicator of learning and an effective means of reinforcing it over time. Of course that assumes the tests are well constructed. The ability to create good tests is a skill that comes with time. There is more to test construction than I will cover in this chapter so I recommend the reader to several references on the subject (Walvoord & Anderson, 2010). However, while we're on the subject, one very helpful tool in developing a good test comes from Bloom's taxonomy of educational objectives. Let's look at an example:

Content Outline	Knowledge	Comprehension	Application	Analysis	Synthesis	Evaluation	Total
History of Adolescence	5	2	1				8
Physical Development	9	4	2	2		2	19
Psychological Implications	4	6		1	1	2	14
Cognitive Development	8	4	1	2	3	1	19
Total # of Items	26	16	4	5	4	5	60

This test planning chart would be for an exam in an adolescent psychology course with 60 planned questions. The number of questions could be set based on the anticipated time necessary to take the test and/or the overall grading schema for the course, including all other assessments. For example, if there were to be a total of 300 points for all course assessments for a perfect grade, this test could contribute 60 points toward those 300. Doing so, however, would mean each question could only be worth 1 point, which may be too small for grading the complexity of each answer. The instructor must therefore make decisions about the individual weighting of each test item as well as the overall weighting of the test within the context of all other course assessments.

The left column of the chart lists the major areas of course content the test covers and the top row represents the level of learning associated with Bloom's hierarchy. The numbers in each cell therefore represent the number of test questions planned for each topic by level of learning. This way of test planning is useful to set the test's parameters before even writing the questions. If we look at the balance of questions in this example, we see the History of Adolescence is weighted lower in question number than the rest of the topics, presumably mirroring both the importance of the topic and the amount of instruction devoted to it. The bottom row in the chart represents the number of questions by level of learning, according to Bloom's taxonomy. Here we see a heavier weighting for knowledge and comprehension over the higher levels of synthesis and evaluation. This plan, therefore may represent a first prelim relatively early in a course where the instructor has yet to approach course content in more advanced levels of learning. Those may be assessed later by means other than tests.

This leads us to another critical aspect of an instructor's summative assessment plan: the need to fit the assessment to the kind and level of learning it is intended to measure. Here I will offer an example from personal experience. Let's say I wanted to help you learn how to sail a boat. My goal would be that you could successfully demonstrate sailing upwind, off the wind and down wind. My instruction might include giving you a reading to do with illustrations, accompanied by lecture demonstrations and finally by practice in a boat. When it came time to determine if you passed the course, if all I did was give you a written test, the assessment concern would be to what degree a written test would give me the necessary *evidence* you could successfully achieve my goal: to navigate through a sailing course laid out with the wind coming from a given direction. In this case, a test would be necessary but not sufficient since there would be skills in handling and execution of helm and sail trim not evident in your test responses.

So, in developing a sufficient assessment schema for a course, the first consideration for the instructor is to be very clear they know—and can actually picture—what they are looking for after instruction. In today's language, we refer to these as learning outcomes. It will be difficult for me to make decisions about how I am going to teach something and then assess my students on how well they learned what I intend if I can't specify in measurable terms what I'm eventually looking for in my students' performances. What does a good learning outcome statement look like? Let's start with some poor examples: "I'm going to introduce the concept of osmotic pressure through a PowerPoint presentation." In this case, the statement is from the teacher's frame of reference. It is more a teaching plan (an *input*) than a learning *outcome*.

Here's another one: "Students will come to appreciate the haiku form." Now we are looking at things from the learner's point of view, but the most critical part of a learning outcome statement is the verb. As we said earlier, evaluation requires measurement, otherwise how will you be able to track the development of a student's learning over time, or determine where one student's performance on an assignment is better than another's? In this example, how do you measure *appreciate*? Humanists might argue that it may cheapen the creative process by thinking of it in measurable terms—that doing so introduces the danger of turning all students' work into mechanized, cooky-cutter products. If one were to be very clear what was sought after, I believe it is possible to summatively grade creative works based on measurably stated learning outcome statements. Here are some examples: "*Transform* your observations about literary texts into a compelling argument." and "*Revise* your writing to enhance interest, logical flow, clarity, concision, coherence, and persuasiveness." Fortunately, there are many tools on the web that can help stimulate instructors how to craft effective learning outcome statements that correlate with the levels of Bloom's taxonomy (http://www.cte.cornell.edu/teaching-ideas/designing-your-course/settting-learning-outcomes.html).

Here are other hard science examples of measurable learning outcome statements based on Bloom's hierarchy: "*Describe* the general characteristics of individual food-borne illness causing agents." and, "*Evaluate* the various schemes for detecting microbial agents." Being this specific helps both the teacher in grading consistency and giving feedback, as well as directs the student in what is expected of them. My experience has also been that starting with clear, measurable learning outcomes can also save the instructor in grading time.

Let's turn our discussion to formative assessment. As we introduced earlier, the primary purpose of formative assessment is to guide the student in their learning by indicating what they have successfully achieved, what remains to be achieved and how to close the gap in levels of performance. What is challenging about this aspect of assessment is the time it takes. Given the fact that every student is a unique individual, giving effective feedback to assist their performance ideally must be done individually. A very useful tool here are rubrics. The best rubrics consist of a matrix that list the specific criteria encompassed in an assignment the instructor is looking for as well as descriptors for a range of performance levels. Here is an example:

Syllabus Development Rubric

Criterion	Beginning	Emerging	Exemplary
Course description	instructor name & contact info, class time and location	in addition: course prerequisites (if any) course description	in addition, how the course fits into the larger program/ department curriculum, field, supplemental readings, and resources
Overall tone	distancing, authoritarian	teacher-oriented	student/learning oriented (eg: first person)
Course objectives	not articulated	stated in general, but vague and unmeasurable terms	listed with appropriate, descriptive verbs that lend themselves to measurement and seek higher levels of learning

Criterion	Beginning	Emerging	Exemplary
Course format	vague, or criptic descriptions of course expectations and how class time will be used	mutual role expectations for students and instructor are explained, together with various teaching methods and modes	role expectations and class format are explained in such a way that students understand the underlying rationale and benefits for them
Instructor beliefs & assumptions	little or no accounting of the instructor's teaching philosophy, beliefs or assumptions about learning	section describing the instructor's beliefs or assumptions about teaching and learning that guide the course	well articulated and thought out rationale that includes the values and/ or experiences that guide the instructor's teaching practice
Class schedule	little or no information of what course topics will be covered each week	course topics broken down by class period	fully articulated and logically sequenced course schedule with chronological topics listed for each class, along with reguired readings and preparation necessary from students
Assignments required	course assignments listed but with no due dates	course assignments listed with clear due dates	assignments listed with due dates, with explanation of late policy and other requirements that might affect grades
Academic policies & procedures	little or no information	description of academic integrity policy	information about all pertinent academic policies, including academic integrity, accommodating students with dissabilities, class attendance

Criterion	Beginning	Emerging	Exemplary
Assignments & grading	little or no information about how the students will be graded; whatever information is included reinforces a grade-focus	each graded assignment is clearly described with its relative value towards the overall course grade	each assignment includes descriptions of its rationale for inclusion in the course and what the student should get out of completing it; use of rubrics with quality criteria specified
Alignment	no clear connection between stated course goals/ objectives and assessment schema	some assignments' connection with stated course goals/objectives is apparent	all assignments are linked with a specific course goal/objective and are likely to provide sufficient evidence to adequately assess each goal/ objective
Diversity of teaching & assessment methods	course teaching and assessment methods are similar; eg: all lectures; all tests	evidence the instructor has employed a diverse set of teaching and assessment methods	diverse assessment methods and evidence that the instructor has taken into account the diversity of students in choosing teaching and assessment methods
Assessment frequency	little or very infrequent venues for giving students feedback on their progress in the course	adequate opportunities for students to get feedback on their progress in the course	all course requirements have sufficient means by which the instructor can keep students adequately appraised of their relative learning progress in the course

Criterion	Beginning	Emerging	Exemplary
Opportunities for feedback on the course	students only opportunity to provide input on their experiences in the course to the instructor is at the end of the course	instructor has developed and scheduled a mid-semester course evaluation opportunity for the students	students are encouraged to provide the instructor with regular input on their experience in the course throughout the semester

This rubric was designed to both guide students in creating course syllabi as well as the instructor in providing effective feedback to them on their successive drafts. The instructor has broken the assignment into the various criteria intrinsic to the assignment in the left column and then established three levels of performance with relative descriptors for each criterion by performance level. Notice the labels used for the performance levels: Beginning . . . Emerging . . . Exemplary. Some might be tempted to use a judgmental scale instead, like poor, average and excellent. The problem of taking that route has to do with what Carol Dweck has termed "Mindset" (Dweck, 2006). By using an evaluative scale the instructor is reinforcing what Dweck refers to as the "Fixed Mindset" which is based on the notion that intelligence and skill are static, where everyone is compared to everyone else in a deterministic view of the world. By using the beginning —> exemplary scale in a rubric, the instructor is reinforcing more of a developmental, or as Dweck refers to it, a *Growth* mindset, characterized by a belief that intelligence and performance can be developed, that reinforces persistence and resilience in the face of failure.

In my experience working with faculty members, those who have used rubrics for both formative and summative assessment have found its benefits include less time required for the process and fewer student complaints. The key principle in their use is to share the rubric with the students before they begin the assignment so they begin their work with more detailed guidance and a clearer picture of what is expected. If a rubric is used for summative purposes, a point value can be assigned to each level of performance described. Those new to rubrics may find starting with fewer performance levels (three) is easier to construct. If that does not allow for sufficient breadth in scoring, the scale can be increased to five, but keep in mind the necessity of creating discrete performance descriptors for each scale level. Another consideration is longer scales have the potential of introducing more subjectivity in assigning points by the instructor.

My experience with using rubrics has shown they can be very effective when used in a formative way. In smaller classes of under 50 students where written assignments are given, instructors can offer students the opportunity to submit drafts of their assignments to get feedback from the instructor through the rubric. They can then use that feedback in making revisions for their final draft to be graded. A study carried out by the Educational Testing Service (Lipnevich & Smith, 2008) has shown that student performance is enhanced more when their drafts are accompanied by feedback alone without a grade.

In larger classes where grading and giving feedback on multiple versions of written assignments is not practical by one person, enlisting the help of students themselves is one option. There are several variations on this practice: self and peer review. Teachers may be concerned about the potential of bias from having students assess their own work. Several studies have shown that with care in both assignment design and in training students in how to self assess their own work, these concerns can be controlled for (Ross, 2006; Falchikov & Boud, 1989). Studies where students reviewed their peer's work have also supported this practice as well (Nicol, Thomson & Breslin, 2014). If you think about it from a broader perspective, when students graduate from school and take their place in a job, most of their lives they will be continually evaluating both their own work and that of their peers. This is a life-long skill that teachers can help their students develop under guidance while in their classes. An educational system that repeatedly requires students to undertake tasks and assignments set by the instructor to be rewarded by a grade does not reinforce the intrinsic values of those efforts for the students themselves. When you get out of school, there are no teachers as such. Performance is no longer graded as it was within academia. Now the stakes are higher: remain employed and advance in your career. Every assignment a teacher may require of their students should connect to some intrinsic, life-long value for the student. If their experience in undertaking that assignment is focused on satisfying the teacher to be rewarded by a grade, they remain in an extrinsic relationship with that effort because its intrinsic value has been overshadowed by years of schooling experience.

Another consideration in developing a grading schema in a course is the decision to grade on the curve or not. The assessment literature mentions two systems: norm-referenced grading and criterion-referenced grading. Norm-referenced grading is grading on the curve. This is illustrated below:

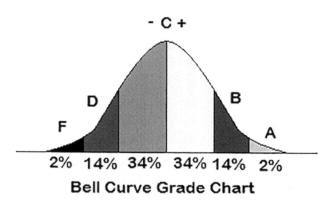

Bell Curve Grade Chart

http://www.calcunation.com/calculators/miscellaneous/bell-curve-grade.php]

Anyone familiar with basic statistics will recognize this graph. When applied to the practice of grading on the curve, it can be used to set grades for individual student's based on their relative performance within a group. In this system, my individual grade is now determined by where my performance falls compared to the other students in my class. Several authors (Walvoord, 2010, pp. 212-123; Svinicki & McKeachie, 2011, pp. 130-131) caution about the disadvantages of this practice. A primary disadvantage is it creates a competitive environment between students. Research on collaborative learning, like that I described in an earlier chapter as used in engineering classes, has shown its positive impact on student learning (Barkley, Cross,& Howell, 2005; Felder, Felder & Dietz, 1998; Michaelsen, Knight & Fink, 2004)).

In contrast to norm-referenced grading, criterion-reference grading is where the teacher sets an absolute performance scale for all students to measure up to regardless of their relative performance to each other. This can be seen in the rubric examples mentioned earlier: to receive the maximum points on an assignment, I must meet the established criteria for that performance standard as set by the instructor. Using this kind of grading schema can reinforce Dweck's notion of growth mindset if students are introduced to a performance standard before undertaking an assignment and then given the opportunity to improve their performance with both detailed feedback from the instructor and repeated performance opportunities. Freshman writing seminars use this system when helping freshman students develop their writing skills through repeated writing assignments that are accompanied by assessment rubrics.

Decisions about using norm-referenced or criterion-referenced grading can be helped by considering the learning environment the instructor believes is most effective for their course (remember our discussion about writing a script for an experience). Students have been programmed over their lives by their experiences with standardized testing. As mentioned earlier, this reinforces a focus on grades (a static performance) over a focus on learning (a dynamic process that happens over time). Teachers must be concerned with how their teaching and assessment decisions affect individual students' levels of confidence in themselves. If a student has adopted a fixed mindset, after repeated experiences of performing at a certain grade level (say a C+), over time they may become tempted to give up too easily and avoid challenges they might learn to overcome which might help them recognize their full potential. If, however, the instructor provides sufficient guidance through feedback and encouragement, like that of a sports coach, students may even outperform their own preconceived limits.

Now let's turn our attention to the need for formative assessment within the class while the instructor is engaged with students. In their book *Classroom Assessment Techniques*, (Angelo & Cross, 1993) the authors present a whole plethora of ways teachers can give and solicit feedback with students to guide instruction and student learning. These techniques serve the fundamental instructional purpose of checking for understanding. They are scripts to structure interactions between teachers and students and between students to make available how everyone is thinking about the class material and their on-going experiences with it and each other. The major challenge for the instructor here is these techniques take time. If the majority of class time is devoted to content delivery, there will be very little opportunity for checking for understanding and the reinforcement of students' integration of that new content. I see this as a function:

The more time you spend delivering content in a class, the less time you have for interaction with students. With the advent of the ever-growing internet, teachers are realizing its liberating effect for content delivery. Those experimenting with flipping their classes are capitalizing on the opportunities to deliver content out of class via course web sites. Using software like Panopto [http://

panopto.com] allows the recording of content delivery through PowerPoint and video clips that can be packaged as on-line modules students review before coming to class. Doing so leaves class time for interactions and activities to help students consolidate that content through application and practice. As mentioned in the earlier chapter on preparing to teach, instructors need to build into their class planning means of determining to what degree their students have achieved the learning outcomes they have set for the class. This means they must budget time for in-class formative (or summative as with graded quizzes) assessment. It is not enough to spend all class time lecturing or delivering content without relying on anything more than non-verbal indicators that they have integrated that content.

Some might argue that it is reasonable to spend class time lecturing and then assessing students' integration of that lecture material later through a summative assessment like a graded exam. The disadvantages of this approach is the students have paid a price with a grade on a performance where the feedback only comes after the grade was assigned. Some research on effective feedback suggests it is more effective when provided sooner after a performance than later (http://perino.pbworks. com/f/Effective+Feedback.pdf), but timing of feedback is context specific. Other studies suggest delaying feedback may be more effective (Butler, Karpicke & Reedier III, 2007). In life after school, most people spend their time performing tasks they both self-assess and get formative feedback on from peers and supervisors before submitting a final version. They are intrinsically motivated in most cases by their own desire to succeed and advance in their work. In the assessment literature, there is recent attention to the concept of *authentic* or *performance assessment*:

> In the [traditional assessment] model, the curriculum drives assessment. "The" body of knowledge is determined first. That knowledge becomes the curriculum that is delivered. Subsequently, the assessments are developed and administered to determine if acquisition of the curriculum occurred. . . . authentic assessments are performance assessments using real-world or authentic tasks or contexts. (http:// jfmueller.faculty.noctrl.edu/toolbox/whatisit.htm)

Therefore, if an instructor was to base their course grading schema on the principles of criterion-referenced and authentic assessment, their students' relationship with the effort they put into their work dramatically changes. They are now more motivated to expend effort to satisfy themselves as a demonstration of their capacity for learning and growth rather than satisfy the teacher in return for an academic artifact like a grade. Things like grade grubbing and cheating become less tempting with the realization that adopting them cheats the learners themselves.

Chapter 6 Principles

1. Subjectivity in grading can be reduced and efficiency increased by the use of rubrics, where appropriate.

2. Before writing test questions, plan the overall test by deciding how many questions for each topic covered as a measure of content emphasis, and deciding how many questions for each level of learning based on Bloom's hierarchy.

3. When Planning what kind of assessment for a specific course outcome, consider what kind of evidence will be necessary to assess it: skill development requires a different kind of evidence from cognitive understanding and development of abstract concepts and from attitude and values changes.

4. Learning outcome statements must be measurable to be assessed. The verbs in the statements can help specify measurability.

5. When using rubrics, student performance can be enhanced by sharing the rubric with them before they complete the assignment.

6. Student learning and performance can be enhanced by incorporating peer evaluation as part of formative assessment.

7. Giving students the opportunity to improve performance through multiple assignment drafts can lead to improved

student work and learning and better prepares them for the world beyond academia.

8. Awareness of learning during class, both for students and by the instructor, can be increased through periodic in-class formative assessments.

References

Angelo, T. A., & Cross, K. P. (1993). *Classroom assessment techniques* (2nd ed.). San Francisco: Jossey-Bass

Barkely, E. F., Cross, K. P., & Howell M. C. (2005). *Collaborative learning techniques: A handbook for college faculty.* San Francisco: Jossey-Bass.

Butler, A. C., Karpicke, J. D.; Roediger, H. L. (2007). The effect of type and timing of feedback on learning from multiple-choice tests. *Journal of Experimental Psychology: Applied, 13*(4). Retrieved from http://dx.doi.org/10.1037/1076-898X.13.4.273

Falchikov, N., & Boud, D. (1989). Student self-assessment in higher education: A meta-analysis. *Review of Educational Research, 59*(4), 395-430.

Felder, R. M., Felder, G. N., & Dietz, E. J. (1998). A longitudinal study of engineering student performance and retention. V. Comparisons with traditionally-taught students. *Journal of Engineering Education, 87*(4), 3-5. Retrieved from http://www4.ncsu.edu/unity/lockers/users/f/felder/public/Papers/long5.html

Huba, M.E., & Freed, J.E. (2000). *Learner-centered assessment on college campuses.* Boston: Allyn & Bacon

Lipnevich, A. A. & Smith, J. K. (2008). *Response to assessment feedback: The effects of grades, praise, and source of information.* Princeton, NJ: Educational Testing Service.

Michaelsen, L. K., Knight, A. B., & Fink, L. D. (Eds.) (2004). *Team-based learning: A transformative use of small groups in college teaching.* Sterling, VA: Stylus.

Nicol, D, Thomson, A., & Breslin, C (2014) Rethinking feedback practices in higher education: A peer review perspective. *Assessment & Evaluation in Higher Education, 39*(1), 102-122.

Ross, J. (2006). The reliability, validity and utility of self-assessment. *Practical Assessment Research & Evaluation, 11*(10), 1-13.

Stevens, D. D., & Antonia J. L. (2005). *Introduction to rubrics: An assessment tool to save grading time, convey effective feedback and promote student learning.* Sterling. VA: Stylus

Suskie, L. (2009). *Assessing student learning.* San Francisco: Jossey-Bass

Svinicki, M, & McKeachie, W. (2011). *McKeachie's teaching tip: Strategies, research, and theory for college and university teachers* (13th ed.). Belmont, CA: Wadsworth.

Walvoord, B. E. F., & Anderson, V. J. (1998). *Effective grading: A tool for learning and assessment.* San Francisco: Jossey-Bass.

Chapter 7
Professional Development: Documenting and Measuring Progress

This chapter is devoted to helping any higher education faculty member develop a plan to document and thereby provide evidence that measures development in teaching. We will base this discussion on the following framework shown in Figure 1 on the next page.

Over a faculty member's career, he or she will develop and accumulate many documents and engage in regular events to continually update their teaching practice and materials. Following from Carol Dweck's idea of a growth mindset, I believe it is helpful to think in terms of skills that can be improved with careful attention and time for experimentation. This framework, therefore distinguishes four discrete skills associated with teaching. Earlier chapters of this book address some of the knowledge and principles of these skill areas, including preparing to teach, creating effective learning experiences and assessment of student learning. If we go back to the anecdote I shared in Chapter one about Steve, the biology TA who aspired to be flamboyant like Johnny Carson, we remember that each of us, as a unique individual will seek our own path to developing our teaching and over time, we will thereby have established our own personal style of teaching. Considering Parker Palmer's recognition that "we teach who we are", if we looked at five separate teachers all teaching the same course, in a sense, we would experience five different courses as they manifest the individual styles and identities of each instructor.

I want to re-emphasize the point I made earlier in Chapter One,

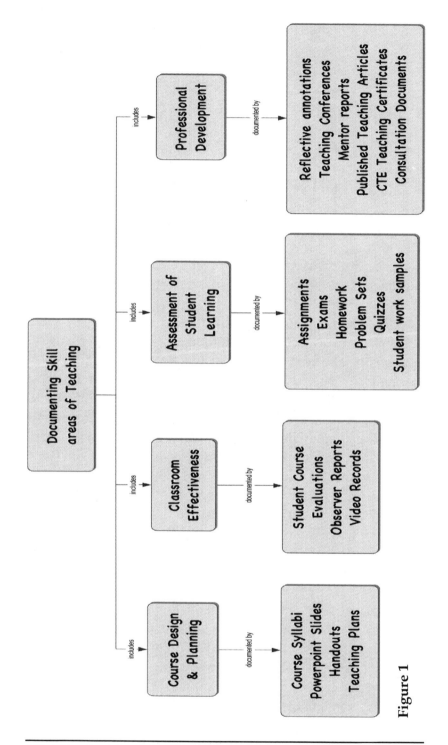

Figure 1

that this fact is liberating—it means we don't all have to do things the same way, and that if we try certain methods and approaches that turn out not to fit with who we are, we are free to seek ones that we feel more at home with. I present this framework as well to recognize that during a faculty member's career, there will be critical milestones where they will be evaluated and reviewed by both students, peers and supervisors that will require evidence of effectiveness and the ability to overcome problems that arise. If we picture a career timeline that begins with the individual's first higher education teaching experiences as a graduate student teaching assistant, and extend that timeline through getting their first academic faculty appointment, and further though the process of achieving tenure, to post-tenure activities that encompass time spent on service to their department, field, college and institution we have identified where those milestones may arise.

So, why does this framework include these four skill areas? I will begin by reviewing one of the most prevalent means of evaluating teaching effectiveness used throughout higher education the world over: end-of-term student evaluation surveys. It is interesting to consider the history of the use of these surveys since they began to be used (Centra, '93; Wachtel, 1998). They began to be used widely in higher education in the late 1960s and early 1970s to assist the instructor in the improvement of teaching practice. Over time they have become a primary data source for making tenure and promotion decisions. The problem with this practice becomes evident when we consider what end-or-term student evaluation surveys actually measure. Based on sample survey questions and considering when they are administered, I believe they have a strong bias towards the students' in-class experience with the instructor, which is where the students have spent the most time to make their judgments when filling out the surveys. Not all students take the time to get to know their instructors outside the classroom such as coming to office hours. Those students who do show up for office hours may carry their own biases if they are doing badly and are in more of a crisis mode and those biases may skew their survey responses.

In contrast, consider how much more time a faculty member spends devoted to teaching that is outside of the classroom and not open to the direct purview of students: the amount of time they spend planning to teach (skill area #1) and how much time and consideration they spend assessing their students' learning (skill area #3—remember our discussion in the last chapter about the time required in providing formative feedback to individual students?) If one was to make the case for effective instructional development over a period of time, input from students that focuses on skill area #2 above is necessary, but not sufficient. There are certain areas of an instructor's teaching that students are neither qualified to evaluate, like the currency of the subject matter (skill area #1), nor sufficiently objective to evaluate, like the means by which they were themselves evaluated (skill area #3). This is not to say that students don't have their own opinions about these areas, but other, more objective and appropriate sources of input on those skills involves the process of peer review of teaching by faculty colleagues.

This raises the question of how best to both administer student surveys of teaching and to interpret the data they generate as both an effective feedback course and means of documenting improvement over time. In the United States, research began in the 1920s and 1930s that looked into the issues of reliability and validity of student evaluations of teaching as well as the degree to which they had an impact on teaching performance. Since then there have been thousands of studies in this area (Arreola, 2007). Based on that research, here are some basic principles to guide their effective use. The first has to do with the relationship between teaching and learning. Student evaluations of teaching, or SETs as they have been referred to in some of the literature, consist of a set of questions focusing on characteristics that contribute to student learning course material. When one considers all the factors that may govern a student's learning, it becomes clear that they extend beyond the influence of the teacher. Therefore, a proper focus in developing SET questions should be *learning* over teaching. Here are some examples to make this clear: "The teacher stimulated interest in the subject matter." That question focuses on the teacher but may not account for the diversity of student characteristics that challenge a teacher to stimulate all of them. A teacher may try to stimulate interest in their students, but some students may be out of reach, especially if it is a required course. We all would agree that stimulating interest in the subject is an important component to their learning, however. So a more effective question would focus more on what contributes to learning the subject that includes teacher characteristics but goes beyond the teacher's input. Here is such a question: "With regard to your learning, what are the most effective components and activities of this course and why?" Here one could include a list of such components for students to select that the instructor has purposely emphasized to both orient the students in their survey responses and to provide more useful, constructive feedback. Such a list might include items like the course web site, the text, laboratory experiments, grading policies, assignments, on-line discussions, and use of class time. An example of a more learning-focused SET can be downloaded here: http://www.cte.cornell.edu/teaching-ideas/designing-your-course/student-evaluations.html. Current practice suggests using SETs much earlier than the end of a course so the input provided can be used by the instructor in time to make necessary modifications. This begs the question of how to interpret and respond to SET-generated data.

Assuming the questions have been validated and are clear to the students, most surveys have two kinds of questions: those that can be quantitatively measured as on a rating scale, and those that are qualitative where the students write a response. In order for any individual response to be significant and useful, it must be representative of a general theme within the group of students. Outlying positive and negative responses may have less to do with the teacher's efforts and more to do with the specific student's state of mind and emotional make-up. One useful practice is to review the quantitative data and focus on the highest and lowest quantitative scores to determine strengths and areas for necessary improvement respectively. Qualitative comments can be grouped by theme and word analysis again to sort out strengths and areas needing development.

If a SET is used in this way as an early feedback system to give students a sense of input and contribution to their experience with an instructor and course, results should be discussed with the class and distinctions made between those matters that are negotiable for modification and those that are not. This will require the instructor to budget class time to engage the students in that conversation so that they recognize their input has been heard and is being taken into account.

Faculty peers are another relevant and potentially useful source of input on instructional effectiveness. Peer mentoring and classroom observations are becoming more and more common not only for new faculty members, but for anyone who seeks to resolve instructional issues. Choosing a mentor or working in a mentoring relationship is an important consideration. There are several aspects to consider in working with a mentor:

- working on communication
- building the relationship
- creating sufficient space and time
- setting mutual expectations and devising a plan to achieve goals
- working towards self-sufficiency
- being aware of power dynamics and identity

After securing a faculty position new hires may be offered the opportunity to work with a mentor. This may represent either a departmental or institutional practice. Some mentoring practices may be more formal and be based on explicit goals and purposes, but many may be more informal and ad hoc. In any case, it will be important to learn the norms of a new departmental culture one has been selected into. Avoiding common mistakes and pitfalls will be mutually important to both parties. A good mentor can help a colleague achieve career goals and feel of value within the department faculty. A well conceived mentoring program can benefit both mentee and mentor (Schrodt, Cawyer & Sanders, 2003).

From a teaching point of view, a new hire will want to learn how their teaching will be evaluated and what policies exist to guide that practice. Questions that could be profitably addressed with a mentor include: are there commonly agreed upon criteria for evaluating teaching within that discipline or faculty culture? How are annual reviews carried out? Is there an effective peer review of teaching process that involves classroom observations? What resources exist within the institution to support instructional effectiveness that are independent of the department, like a teaching support center? The type of institution will determine much of these matters. Large research universities may require newly hired tenure-track faculty members to spend the first year or even longer establishing their research program before adding much in the way of teaching responsibilities. In more teaching-oriented institutions, newly hired faculty may be required to document their teaching through a portfolio or teaching dossier. A final consideration in both choosing and working with a faculty mentor is the scope of the focus of the relationship. As was pointed out in chapter one, everyone has a unique identity and background. Working with the whole person, as opposed to working with just the academic part of them may play a critical role when considerations of personal versus professional matters are at stake.

Besides these considerations for how others may evaluate an instructor's teaching there is the primary matter of how one documents and evaluates one's own teaching, which I consider a discrete skill in itself. Since the most time of teaching is spent on preparation and assessment of student learning, those areas should be addressed thoroughly. With all the other demands for their time, a busy academic will want to be efficient both in how they prepare for teaching and how they grade and provide sufficient feedback to students. These are discrete skills and therefore will require different approaches and measures to monitor skill development. At the lowest level of the framework pictured earlier are the documents that are generated over time for each skill area to track its development. Reviewing earlier drafts of course syllabi and teaching plans and tracking changes that are made with experience is a way to document one's course design and class planning skills—skill area 1. We've discussed the use of student evaluations of teaching, particularly if used part-way through a semester to track improvements in the classroom experience students have—skill area 2, but there are additional means of documenting that skill including peer observers and video records made of one's classes by staff in teaching centers.

Development in assessment practices—skill area 3—can be documented by tracking improvements in assignment design, exam construction and in samples of student work, both collectively for a course from one semester to the next and individually for students within a semester. If one saves samples of student work to share with others in any kind of evaluative review process, the instructor must get the permission of the student, and remove any identifying information so that student remains anonymous. As a separate skill area, professional development can be documented through several means and activities. I have written on this extensively elsewhere (Way, Teaching Evaluation Handbook: http://www.cte.cornell.edu/documents/Teaching%20 Evaluation%20Handbook.pdf). Over the past 40 years higher education institutions have invested increasingly in supporting their faculty members' teaching development. Evidence for this can be seen in the number of teaching and learning centers throughout higher educational institutions world-wide (http://podnetwork. org/publications/google-custom-search-of-center-web-sites/) as well as the ever-growing on-line resources available (http:// www.developfaculty.com/online/index.html). In addition are the number of journals devoted to the exchange of scholarly work on higher education teaching and learning (https://www.seattleu.edu/ faculty-development/resources/journals/). Many disciplines have their own journals devoted to teaching and learning as well as conference sessions devoted to teaching and learning by discipline.

Possible means of documenting teaching development over time include attendance at pedagogically-oriented events—both on and off campus, publication of articles on teaching methods, research on instructional effectiveness, use of instructional development resources, participation in peers' instructional development, mentoring and serving on teaching evaluation teams. A sampling of Cornell's Center for Teaching Excellence programs includes mini-grants to support professional development and instructional innovation, regular faculty seminars on teaching and learning approaches, certificate programs to help participating faculty members document their participation in center-sponsored events, mid-semester student evaluation of teaching support, individual, confidential consultations about teaching effectiveness and opportunities for class observations and video recordings followed up with debriefings by center staff. Regardless of whether you elect to engage with any of these many resources and opportunities, over a teaching career you will continually take steps and invest time in developing your teaching as was discussed in chapter 2. Considering that most higher education faculty members are involved with their own scholarly and research work, being efficient and saving time in one's own teaching development efforts is a major consideration. Let's go back to a suggestion I made in chapter 2: to keep a teaching journal. Regardless of your past journaling experiences or concern about the time required to keep one, the fact is our memories are limited, especially when our days and weeks are jammed with a myriad of responsibilities, events and stressors. We'd all like to shorten the time it takes to improve practice and skill. That time is lengthened when we continually forget subtle things we learn on a daily basis from trial and error and therefore keep making similar mistakes until they become sufficiently imprinted on our memories to overcome the problems we face. My argument is that the time required for keeping a teaching journal may be less than the time saved from the lessons learned from the effort.

As I have written earlier (Way, 2012), for faculty members to effectively document instructional development, measurable changes over time are necessary. Discussion of experimental approaches, their modification based on feedback and how best to document effective improvement is where peer collaboration can be of help, particularly when the peers are knowledgeable in the course content. Documenting such collaboration and measurable changes over time should be a major focus within a teaching evaluation process. (Way, '02: http://www.publications.hr.uwa.edu.au/iced2002/iced2002/abstracts/santhanam). Here are some possible criteria for an instructor to monitor professional development during their career:

Professional Development of Self and others

- To what extent did the instructor actively seek out feedback from colleagues on classroom pedagogy, assignment development and/or grading?
- To what extent did the instructor seek out information on pedagogy from outside sources such as conferences, consultation services, texts and articles for incorporation into teaching?
- To what extent did the instructor coach or support colleagues on classroom pedagogy, assignment development and/or grading?
- To what extent did the instructor generate and disseminate information on pedagogy through conferences, texts and articles?
- To what extent did the instructor occasionally sit in on colleagues' classes with follow-up constructive discussion
- To what extent did the instructor seek out feedback from students, peers, and others, identify problem areas, experiment with ways of improving his/her teaching such that problems were eliminated/minimized?
- To what extent did the instructor engage in activities designed to improve teaching (e.g., presentations on teaching at professional meetings, using instructional development resources on and off campus)?
- To what extent did the instructor regularly meet with colleagues to discuss teaching issues, problems, offer ideas, share techniques and/or review teaching materials?

- To what extent has the instructor provided evidence from these activities that show sustained development of teaching quality over time?

Whether one is evaluating one's own teaching development or going through a review process where others are doing the evaluating, having strong, reliable and compelling evidence of teaching development will be necessary to improve the validity of that evaluation as well as to save time in the process for all involved. For over twenty years a common practice for effectively developing one's teaching and for documenting that development for review by others has been the teaching portfolio (Seldin, 1999; Edgerton, Hutchings & Quinlan, 1991). What is a teaching portfolio and how can it serve both of these purposes? If one thinks of an artist's portfolio and how it might be used, several criteria come to mind: it will represent both the range of skills the artist has, for example, oil paintings, pastel drawings, watercolors, commercial work, illustrations as well as personal expression, while at the same time provide exemplary samples of each of those areas of work. As a professional gains more experience over time, earlier exemplars may be replaced by more contemporary ones, so the portfolio is ever-changing and being updated to represent best work. Freelance artists will bring a portfolio to a prospective employer who may want to contract for that artist's work to remain gainfully employed.

In the same way, a teacher will want to package their developed materials that both represent the range of skills they have as an instructor as well as to provide evidence of successful practice for both seeking employment and in remaining employed. Portfolios in academia have been employed long enough to generalize a common structure as illustrated below in Figure 2.

Reviewing the framework offered at the beginning of this chapter that includes the four major skill areas of teaching, as they apply to a teaching portfolio, we can see where the documents listed in each of the four skill areas would represent work samples, or artifacts of teaching the instructor has developed through

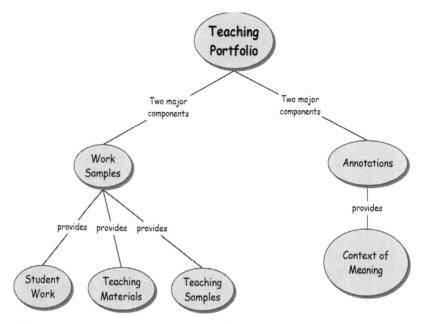

Figure 2

practice over time. The second, and most critical component of a teaching portfolio consists of reflective annotations of each artifact the instructor has chosen to represent a skill's development. There are several reasons these reflective annotations are the most critical part of the portfolio. The first has to do with the fact that a portfolio is not merely a product or object, but it is also a dynamic process that represents one's teaching work over time. Just as the artist will continually update their portfolio over time to reveal improvement in skill and development of personal style, so a teacher will want to benchmark stages of teaching practice as their experiences expand and their career unfolds. They will want to do this both for their own sense of accomplishment as well as to provide evidence to others that they are capable of continual development and remaining current in practice as things evolve.

In anybody's busy day and weeks subtle but important aspects of experience are lost to memory. Going back to our earlier discussion about the importance of reflection in chapter 2, an instructor will want to capitalize on lessons learned through practice by making records of those lessons for future reference. This is most easily seen after teaching a class, and at the end of a course. Without some kinds of records to keep track of things, one's learning curve may be unnecessarily flatter. Thus, the portfolio is a place where these notes to one's self can be further refined as working principles for the future and articulated in the reflective annotations accompanying each teaching artifact chosen for inclusion. What do the trends in student evaluation comments mean for making changes in one's teaching plans or course design decisions? What new texts or research articles come along that inspire ideas for changes in course readings? What conversations with colleagues or department heads will be important to recall for making career choices? What non-academic experiences like travel and personal contacts and relationships may stimulate insights into improved practices? In the absence of making even cryptic records of these events, much of the value and richness of our lives may be lost to memory. Even things we think we'll never forget will lose their luster and detail as time goes by. This can become very evident and vivid if one were to read old letters written or received in the past, watch old videos of past events and experiences and become thereby reminded of what has become dim over time. This is where keeping a teaching journal may really pay off. Each entry represents a moment in time. Reviewing entries logged over long periods of months and years can reveal closely held values and beliefs as well as risks taken when new opportunities arise. Decisions made for changes made act as benchmarks to evaluate their effectiveness.

Besides the value to one's self of these reflective annotations, they will be very valuable to anyone else reading them—like a prospective employer, a department chair in an annual review, or a tenure review committee. Since everyone's time is limited and therefore precious, those that one chooses or is required to share a teaching portfolio with may not be able to review everything. The annotations that accompany the included artifacts help an outside audience, like a reviewer, understand the developmental context of each artifact. Reviewing them can act as a way of understanding the instructor's historical development in each area of skill. Here is a set of prompts that might assist the instructor in articulating the reflective artifacts in each of the suggested teaching skill areas:

Course Design & Planning for Instruction:

What guides you in selecting the artifacts included here? What is unique in how you plan? How have you worked on becoming efficient in your teaching prep time? What rationale has guided you in the design of the courses you've included syllabi of?

Assessing Student Learning & Providing effective feedback:

This section serves to document your evolving practices of grading students. Do they include self- and peer-assessment? How do they help your students for life after academia? Do you utilize authentic assessment assignments? What kinds of evidence of learning are you aiming for in your assignments? This is also where you can illustrate how you interact with your students by giving them the feedback they need to improve their work. Do you use rubrics? Do you have examples of student work you can include? How do you use office hours, e-mail, course web sites, technology?

Creating Effective classroom learning experiences:

This is where you can document your evolving practices of teaching and learning strategies—how do you use class time? How do you connect in- and out-of-class time? How do you get feedback from your students on course design & your teaching? When do you seek that feedback (i.e. through mid-term student evaluations?) How do you use that information? This is also where you can summarize your students' feedback over time and for various kinds of courses yo teach and keep a record of modifications you've made to your teaching practice through the analysis of student feedback.

Professional Development:

What is our professional development plan? How will you continually develop your research? Your teaching? Where does mentoring fit in? What role does your portfolio have in your teaching development?

Finally, some principles to guide the instructor in what to include in the portfolio and in making decisions to periodically update it will be helpful. The following diagram (see Figure 3 on the following page) may help as a starting place.

We've explored the criterion of representativeness in the four skill areas discussed and that of reflectiveness in the description of the reflective annotations. The issue of purpose raises other considerations that must be explored. As was pointed out earlier, there will be critical milestones throughout any academic career that may govern the use and purpose of the portfolio in each stage. Having exemplary materials to represent one's teaching development all included and structured in one place will be very helpful, particularly if they are in digital form as on a password-controlled web site to facilitate sharing with selected reviewers throughout the world. What one will have at the outset of a career will reflect that stage of experience and development and serve in a teaching job search. After employment in a faculty position, the portfolio may or may not be explicitly required, depending on the type of institution and role teaching plays in that job. With more years of experience and seniority in a teaching career, the artifacts will change to reflect added skill and professional interests. These changes will need to be reflected in the decision about what is included and how the portfolio is structured because the portfolio's purpose and use will be a reflection of those changes.

This book has been written and organized around the framework noted earlier in this chapter to help higher education faculty early in their careers benefit from some of the literature and research in the area as well as avoid common pitfalls of practice. I have drawn upon both my own experience as a teacher as well as many years observing and consulting with and assisting higher education faculty in a wide range of disciplines including the

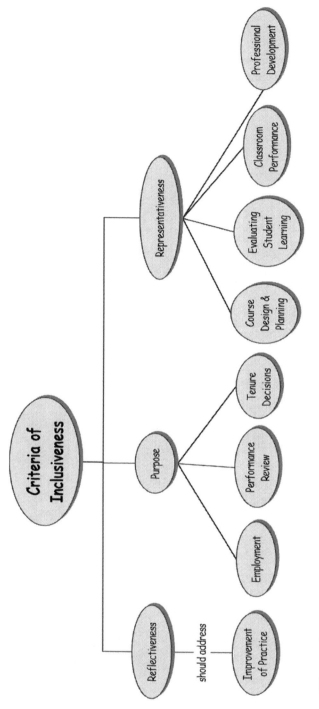

Figure 3

hard and social sciences and the humanities. Where necessary and appropriate I have referenced some of the relevant and useful research not only on effective teaching methods, but also the very promising research on human learning. During a career as a higher education faculty member, you will yourself find practical use of both anecdotes and stories of experiences your colleagues have to share as well as the stream of literature that continues to explore this fascinating and critical human endeavor. My hope is you have found some useful nuggets of both the lore of teaching as well as the wisdom of practice and that as you continue on your pedagogical journey you may be inspired to contribute your own stories and empirical wisdom to that growing body of knowledge and practice. There is much at stake here for all of us.

Principles from Chapter 7

1. Don't wait until the end of a course to solicit feedback from your students on how the course is going, use an early student survey around week five and focus questions on the course components and the degree to which they've contributed to students' learning.
2. Always discuss early course feedback with your students and distinguish between those matters that are negotiable and those that aren't.
3. Seek a faculty mentor early in your career who can help you focus on practical goal setting and monitoring progress.
4. When interviewing for a faculty position, ask questions about how teaching will be evaluated.
5. Once hired, seek out institutional resources on teaching, like teaching centers.
6. Develop an organized system, like a portfolio, to regularly document your teaching's development over time.

References

Arreola, R. (1995). *Developing a comprehensive faculty evaluation system*. Bolton, MA: Anker.

Centra, J. (1993). *Reflective faculty evaluation*. San Francisco: Jossey-Bass.

Edgerton, R., Hutchings, P., & Quinlan, K. (1991). *The teaching portfolio – Capturing the scholarship in teaching*. Washington, DC: American Association for Higher Education.

Schrodt, P., Cawyer, C., & Sanders, R. (2003). An Examination of academic mentoring behaviors and new faculty members' satisfaction with socialization and tenure and promotion processes, *Communication Education*, 52(1), 17-29.

Seldin, P. (1999). *Changing practices in evaluating teaching*. Bolton, MA: Anker.

Wachtel, H. K . (1998). Student evaluation of college teaching effectiveness: A brief review. *Assessment & Evaluation in Higher Education, 23*(2) 191

Way, D. (2012). *Teaching evaluation handbook*. Ithica, NY: Center for Teaching Excellence, Cornell University. Retrieved from [http://www.cte.cornell.edu/documents/Teaching%20Evaluation%20Handbook.pdf].

Bibliography

Angelo, T. A., & Cross, K. P. (1993). *Classroom assessment techniques* (2nd ed.). San Francisco: Jossey-Bass

Argyris, C. & Schon, D. *Theory in practice: Increasing professional effectiveness.* San Francisco: Jossey-Bass, 1974.

Arreola, R. (1995). *Developing a comprehensive faculty evaluation system.* Bolton, MA: Anker.

Asato, M.R., Terwilliger, R., Woo, J., & Luna, B. (2010). White matter development in adolescence: A DTI study. *Cereb Cortex.* 20(9), 2122-31.

Ausubel, D, Novak, J.D, & Hanesian, H. (1978) *Educational psychology – A cognitive view* (2nd ed.). New York: Holt, Rinehart & Winston.

Barkely, E. F., Cross, K. P., & Howell M. C. (2005). *Collaborative learning techniques: A handbook for college faculty.* San Francisco: Jossey-Bass.

Beichner, R. J., Saul, J. M., Abott, D. S., Morse, J. J., Deardorff, D. L., Allain, R. J., Bonham, S. W., Dancy, M. H., & Risley, J. S. (2007). The student-centered activities for large enrollment undergraduate programs (SCALE-UP) project. In E. F. Redish & P. J. Cooney (Eds.), *Research-based reform in university physics* (Vol. 1). College Park, MD: American Association of Physics Teachers. Retrieved October 12, 2009 from http://www.compadre.org/per/per_reviews/volume1.cfm.

Beilock, S. (2010). *Choke – What the secrets of the brain reveal about getting it right when you have to.* New York. Free Press.

Bligh, D.A. (2000). *What's the use of lectures.* San Francisco: Josses-Bass.

Bok, D. (2006). *Our underachieving colleges : A candid look at how much students learn and why they should be learning more.* Princeton, NJ. Princeton University Press.

Bonwell, C., & Eison, J. (1991) *Active learning: Creating excitement in the classroom,* Washington, DC: ASHE-ERIC.

Bronowski, J. (1965). *Science and human values.* New York: Julian Messner.

Brookfield, S. (1995). *Becoming a critically reflective teacher.* San Francisco: Jossey-Bass.

Brown, P.C., Roediger III, H.L. & McDaniel, M.A. (2014). *Make it stick — The science of successful learning.* Cambridge, MA: Harvard University Press.

Butler, A. C., Karpicke, J. D.; Roediger, H. L. (2007). The effect of type and timing of feedback on learning from multiple-choice tests. *Journal of Experimental Psychology: Applied, 13*(4). Retrieved from http://dx.doi.org/10.1037/1076-898X.13.4.273

Carnes, M. (2014). *Minds on fire: How role-immersion games transform college.* Cambridge, MA. Harvard University Press.

Centra, J. (1993). *Reflective faculty evaluation.* San Francisco: Jossey-Bass.

Dweck, C. (2006). *Mindset — The new psychology of success.* New York: Ballantine.

Edgerton, R., Hutchings, P., & Quinlan, K. (1991). *The teaching portfolio — Capturing the scholarship in teaching.* Washington, DC: American Association for Higher Education.

Falchikov, N., & Boud, D. (1989). Student self-assessment in higher education: A meta-analysis. *Review of Educational Research, 59*(4), 395-430.

Felder, R. M., Felder, G. N., & Dietz, E. J. (1998). A longitudinal study of engineering student performance and retention. V. Comparisons with traditionally-taught students. *Journal of Engineering Education, 87*(4), 3-5. Retrieved from http://www4.ncsu.edu/unity/lockers/users/f/felder/public/Papers/long5.html

Gowin. D.B. (1981). *Educating.* Ithaca, NY: Cornell University Press.

Hofstadter, R. (1963). *Anti-intellectualism in American life.* New York: Knopf.

Huba, M.E., & Freed, J.E. (2000). *Learner-centered assessment on college campuses.* Boston: Allyn & Bacon.

Huston, T. (2009). *Teaching what you don't know.* Cambridge, MA: Harvard University Press.

Johnstone, A. H., & Percival, F. (1976). Attention breaks in lectures, *Education in Chemistry, 13*(2), 49-50.

Larkin, J., McDermott, J., Simon, D. P., & Simon, H. A. (1980). Expert and novice performance in solving physics problems. *Science, 208*(4450), 1335-42.

Lipnevich, A. A. & Smith, J. K. (2008). *Response to assessment feedback: The effects of grades, praise, and source of information.* Princeton, NJ: Educational Testing Service.

Michaelsen, L. K., Knight, A. B., & Fink, L. D. (Eds.) (2004). *Team-based learning: A transformative use of small groups in college teaching.* Sterling, VA: Stylus.

Miller, G.A. (1967). The magical number seven, plus or minus two: Some limits on our capacity for processing information. In *The Psychology of Communication.* New York: Penguin.

Nicol, D, Thomson, A., & Breslin, C (2014) Rethinking feedback practices in higher education: A peer review perspective. *Assessment & Evaluation in Higher Education, 39*(1), 102-122.

Olson, R. (2009). *Don't be such a scientist.* Washington, DC: Island Press.

Palmer, P. (1998). *The courage to teach: Exploring the inner landscape of a teacher's life.* San Francisco: Jossey-Bass.

Perry, W (1970). *Forms of intellectual and ethical development in the college years,* San Francisco: Holt Reinhart/Jossey-Bass.

Pedersen, O. (1997). *The first universities.* Cambridge, UK. Cambridge University press.

Ross, J. (2006). The reliability, validity and utility of self-assessment. *Practical Assessment Research & Evaluation, 11*(10), 1-13.

Schön, D. (1983) *The reflective practitioner: How professionals think in action.* New York: Basic Books.

Schrodt, P., Cawyer, C., & Sanders, R. (2003). An Examination of academic mentoring behaviors and new faculty members' satisfaction with socialization and tenure and promotion processes, *Communication Education,* 52(1), 17-29.

Seldin, P. (1999). *Changing practices in evaluating teaching.* Bolton, MA: Anker.

Shulman, L. (1986). Those who understand: Knowledge growth in teaching. *Educational Researcher, 15*(2), 4-14. Washington, DC: The American Educational Research Association.

Steele, C. (2010). *Whistling vivaldi – How stereotypes affect us and what we can do.* New York. Norton.

Stevens, D. D., & Antonia J. L. (2005). *Introduction to rubrics: An assessment tool to save grading time, convey effective feedback and promote student learning. Sterling.* VA: Stylus

Suskie, L. (2009). *Assessing student learning.* San Francisco: Jossey-Bass

Svinicki, M, & McKeachie, W. (2011). *McKeachie's teaching tip: Strategies, research, and theory for college and university teachers* (13th ed.). Belmont, CA: Wadsworth.

Wachtel, H. K. (1998). Student evaluation of college teaching effectiveness: A brief review. *Assessment & Evaluation in Higher Education, 23*(2) 191

Walvoord, B. E. F., & Anderson, V. J. (1998). *Effective grading: A tool for learning and assessment.* San Francisco: Jossey-Bass.

Way, D. (2012). *Teaching evaluation handbook.* Ithica, NY: Center for Teaching Excellence, Cornell University. Retrieved from [http://www.cte.cornell.edu/documents/Teaching%20Evaluation%20Handbook.pdf].

Weimer, M. (2002). *Learner-centered teaching: Five key changes to practice.* San Francisco: Jossey-Bass

Zull, J. E. (2002). *The art of changing the brain.* Sterling, VA: Stylus.

About the Author

In the 40 years since Dr. David Way has been teaching at Cornell University, he has helped initiate college-wide graduate teaching development programs in four colleges, developed training and educational materials used throughout the university, assisted several colleges to redesign their student evaluation of teaching systems, and initiated and published the first university-wide newsletter on undergraduate education. He has consulted with over 40 departments and academic fields on instructional and faculty development, encompassing nine schools and colleges on the Ithaca campus, and has been instrumental in the design and development of an annual faculty retreat on teaching and learning.

David teaches ALS 6015, The Practice of Teaching in Higher Education, and is the author of the *Cornell Teaching Evaluation Handbook.* He has been involved in the University Self-Study Working Group on Assessment of Student Learning and on the Vice Provost for Undergraduate Education's Core Assessment Committee. Other previous projects include: Enhancing teaching in research-intensive environments, an international collaboration through Oxford University, UK, and exploring good leadership and management practice in higher education: issues of engagement, an international collaboration through Cambridge University, UK.

David currently serves as an Associate Director for Cornell University's Center for Teaching Excellence. He is the Center Liaison to the College of Agriculture and Life Sciences, the Cornell Law School and the College of Veterinary Medicine.

Made in the USA
Lexington, KY
23 August 2016